TEACHING SCIENCE IN DIVERSE CLASSROOMS

As a distinctive voice in science education writing, Douglas B. Larkin provides a fresh perspective for science teachers who work to make real science accessible to all K-12 students. Through compelling anecdotes and vignettes, this book draws deeply on research to present a vision of successful and inspiring science teaching that builds upon the prior knowledge, experiences, and interests of students. With empathy for the challenges faced by contemporary science teachers, *Teaching Science in Diverse Classrooms* encourages teachers to embrace the intellectual task of engaging their students in learning science, and offers an abundance of examples of what high-quality science teaching for all students looks like.

Divided into three sections, this book is a connected set of chapters around the central idea that the decisions made by good science teachers help light the way for their students along both familiar and unfamiliar pathways to understanding. The book addresses topics and issues that occur in the daily lives and career arcs of science teachers such as:

- Aiming for culturally relevant science teaching
- Eliciting and working with students' ideas
- Introducing discussion and debate
- Reshaping school science with scientific practices
- Viewing science teachers as science learners

Grounded in the Next Generation Science Standards (NGSS), this is a perfect supplementary resource for both preservice and inservice teachers and teacher educators that addresses the intellectual challenges of teaching science in contemporary classrooms and models how to enact effective, reform-based science teaching practices for all students while working within real-world constraints.

Douglas B. Larkin is an Associate Professor in the Department of Teaching and Learning at Montclair State University. He has worked as a high school science teacher and educator in New Jersey, Wisconsin, Kenya, and Papua New Guinea. His research examines science teacher preparation and retention, as well as issues of equity and justice in teacher education.

"This book speaks to all types of science teachers and their different contexts—Doug Larkin is writing to a diverse science teacher audience. The way he integrates and weaves together stories from his teaching and his work as a teacher educator with those of other teachers makes the whole book feel connected, an authentic learning experience. The book is written the same way he envisions science teaching—it is meant to be intriguing and *real* not just a series of facts forced onto the reader."

Anna Monteiro, Ph.D., Program Officer,
Knowles Teacher Initiative

"I love the tempo and approach to this book. It is accessible and clearly connects the 'bigger issues' of science education to the actual practices of teaching."

Dr. David Meshoulam, Co-Founder and Executive
Director of Speak for the Trees and High-School
and College Science Instructor

"As a (former) science teacher I felt both validated and challenged by the book. It is a wonderfully realistic portrayal of teaching science in real classrooms and recognition of all that science teaching entails. I like that Larkin encourages teachers to forge stronger connections to science practices and deeper learning, and he communicates these important messages as a nudge towards more collaborative sense-making. It's positive and encouraging and offers teachers ways to reorient what they already do towards more robust science teaching."

Jennifer Wilfrid, Senior Outreach Specialist, WIDA at the
Wisconsin Center for Education Research

TEACHING SCIENCE IN DIVERSE CLASSROOMS

Real Science for Real Students

Douglas B. Larkin

Routledge
Taylor & Francis Group

NEW YORK AND LONDON

First published 2020
by Routledge
52 Vanderbilt Avenue, New York, NY 10017

and by Routledge
2 Park Square, Milton Park, Abingdon, Oxon OX14 4RN

Routledge is an imprint of the Taylor & Francis Group, an informa business

© 2020 Taylor & Francis

Library of Congress Cataloging-in-Publication Data
A catalog record for this title has been requested

ISBN: 978-0-367-18995-2 (hbk)
ISBN: 978-0-367-18997-6 (pbk)
ISBN: 978-0-429-19972-1 (ebk)

Typeset in Bembo
by Taylor & Francis Books

MIX
Paper from
responsible sources
FSC
www.fsc.org
FSC® C013985

Printed in the United Kingdom
by Henry Ling Limited

For Melissa, Casey, and Amani

CONTENTS

ACKNOWLEDGMENTS

This book would not have been possible without the assistance of many people, and I am grateful to all of them. I wish to express my appreciation to those who helped me flesh out the ideas in this book as I worked on them, including my doctoral students Nellista Bess, Jayne Tanis, William Brown, Ted Graham, Catherine Gaynor, Karen Woodruff, Liz Carletta, and Suzanne Poole. I also wish to thank Sherry Southerland, Lama Jaber, Miray Tekkumru-Kisa, and all of the wonderful science education students at Florida State University—with extra gratitude to Kirby Whittington, whose questions drove me to write the opening chapter as she drove me around Tallahassee.

Special thanks to Mary Ellin Logue, Timothy Reagan and Tammy Mills for the opportunity to serve as the Visiting Libra Professor at the University of Maine College of Education and Human Development, during my sabbatical in the fall of 2017. I also wish to thank Asli Senzen-Barrie, Patrick Womac, Justin Dimmel, Bryan Silverman, Elizabeth Hufnagel, Erin Straine, John Maddeus, Natasha Speer, and Camden Bock and the rest of the fantastic faculty and students in Orono.

I would also like to express my appreciation to all of my colleagues at Montclair State University, including Dean Tamara Lucas, and all of the colleagues I have worked with on the science education projects referenced in this book, including Sandra Adams, Sumi Hagiwara, Tanya Maloney, Mayida Zaal, Emily Klein, Monica Taylor, Jackie Willis, Susan Moore Taylor, Jennifer Robinson, Vanessa Klein, Bill Thomas, Randy FitzGerald, Linda Abrams, and Jennifer Correa-Kruegel, as well as my colleagues in the Department of Secondary and Special Education and the College of Education and Human Services. Nicole Barnes gets her own special thank you. Sue Baglieri does too.

Many thanks to John Settlage, Heidi Carlone, David Stroupe, John Rudolph, and Ana Maria Villegas as touchstones for my sanity throughout this project.

I am especially appreciative to early readers of various drafts of this book (and writing that made its way into this book) who gave valuable feedback, including Bill Bigelow, Don Drott, Anna-Karina Monteiro, Jennifer Wilfrid, Katelyn Farrar, Lindsay Oliver, and David Meshoulam. I am grateful once more to work on a creative endeavor with Steve Spatucci, who read and gave feedback on an early draft (very early if Science Geek issues #1–5 count), and designed the cover for the paperback edition. An earlier version of Chapter 10 first appeared in Rethinking Schools magazine (fall 2011, Vol. 26 #1) and in Bill Bigelow and Tim Swinehart, eds., A People's Curriculum for the Earth: Teaching Climate Change and the Environmental Crisis, Rethinking Schools, 2015. An earlier version of Chapter 12, originally appeared as, "10 things to know about mentoring student teachers" in Phi Delta Kappan in April 2013. Thanks to Karen Adler for bringing this book to Routledge, Simon Jacobs for seeing it through to publication, George MacBeth for copy-editing, and Helen Chomyszyn for the final stages of production.

Truly, this book would not have been possible without the ongoing cooperation of science teachers across the country who have let me into their classrooms over the years—you have my deepest respect, and I hope I have represented you well here.

My greatest thanks go to my family. My parents, John and Barbara have been supportive at every turn, and my mom's top-notch editing skills have improved this book immeasurably (though of course, any errors that remain within are mine). Finally, I wish to thank Melissa, Casey, and Amani for their support and love all along the way. This book is dedicated to them.

This material is based upon work supported by the National Science Foundation under Grant No. 1339956. Any opinions, findings and conclusions or recommendations expressed in this material are those of the author and do not necessarily reflect the views of the National Science Foundation (NSF).

INTRODUCTION

Teaching Real Science to Real Students: On Being a Thoughtful Science Teacher and Doing a Good Job

The category of people who call themselves science teachers—and I include myself among them—is filled with thoughtful individuals who sincerely want to do a good job in teaching science to students. As science teachers, we want our students to solve problems, think critically, and have a depth of understanding about big scientific ideas and important science practices. We also take seriously our responsibility to the scientific community to ensure that generations of hard-won knowledge gets passed along to the future with fidelity. Many of us cannot resist cultivating in our students the same sense of wonder about the world that we ourselves feel when we are engaged in science. And we think long and hard about the reasons why first-rate science teaching is not happening everywhere and for all students.

For most, teaching science means ensuring that students gain a deep understanding of the big ideas that have helped human beings to shape the world in which we now live. For many, teaching science also means trying to level the playing field so that students in resource-poor communities have access to the same learning opportunities as those in more well-off places. In some schools, the reasons for learning science are intimately linked to community issues of environmental justice, while in others science is framed as simply one component of a well-rounded education. In some elementary and middle schools, science is highly-valued as a vehicle for literacy and mathematics instruction, while other places emphasize the creative aspects of scientific inquiry and attend to the ways in which scientific knowledge is generated in the first place. In many cases, the grades that students earn in science classes become a currency that can be later exchanged for class rank, college credit, and future employment.

Out of necessity, real science and school science are not always the same thing; science is a vast and sprawling enterprise, and transforming it into school science is part of an effort to make scientific knowledge accessible and understandable to young minds.[1] Science embodies a way of thinking about the world that uses empirical evidence as the basis for knowing, yet it is often taught in schools in ways that compel students to rely on the authority of teachers, or at least a "right" answer written down somewhere. Real science is messy and uncertain, with lots of false starts, dead ends, and noisy data. By contrast, school science is often neatly divided into textbook chapters, sub-topics, and bite-sized bits of information that can be efficiently assessed by teachers. Real science is as much concerned with asking questions as it is with answering them, while much of school science still focuses on recalling facts and solving problems. The exceptions of course, are in classrooms where teachers have made room for students' own thinking, where the spirit of inquiry thrives.

★★★

Though thousands share the job description of "science teacher," many have very different experiences in their work lives, and the range of issues faced by teachers in schools reflects the diverse nature of their employment. Even just within the United States, the variety in these situations is breathtaking. Here are a few examples of the types of schools and contexts in which science teachers work—informed by real examples of places I have encountered in my own research and practice as a teacher educator:

- A school that is sufficiently resourced, with functioning laboratory spaces and annual departmental budgets for ordering supplies, that also has an underlying cheating epidemic driven by high-stakes testing.
- A middle school in a high-poverty urban neighborhood that has a robust science department led by a team of charismatic and collaborative teachers, who continue to find ways to make every student want to learn science.
- A rural school that struggles to hold onto its agricultural science program in the face of a changing population with little experience or prospects in farming.
- A magnet school that focuses on science and technology, where the degree of teacher autonomy is rivaled only by an exhausting range of instructional quality.
- An elementary school where teachers gladly trade autonomy for confidence in their own teaching by using science kits; where a small minority of teachers modify directions and repurpose the materials to give their students a more authentic experience with scientific inquiry.

There are science classrooms within walking distance of one another that might as well exist in parallel universes, because the work of science teaching and learning is so different in each. Yet the underlying mission for every science teacher—even taking into account the local curriculum and state standards—can be stated quite simply: in teaching science, how do I meet my students where they are?

★★★

There are many books about teaching science that are full of lesson plans, activities, science demonstrations, and collections of tips and tricks. I love those books, and have leaned heavily on them in my teaching, but this is not one of them. Rather, this is a book about the intellectual work of science teaching, undertaken by teachers for the purpose of shaping the subject matter they know and love for the specific students they teach. It is a connected set of essays orbiting loosely around the idea that the decisions made by good science teachers help light the way for their students along both familiar and unfamiliar pathways to understanding. Deeply embedded in the genome of this book are the principles and ideas from the Next Generation Science Standards, as well as ongoing research in science education and science teacher education.[2]

As a job, science teaching has been needlessly constrained by widely-held, impoverished conceptions about teaching, which view it as the controlled delivery of information from teacher to student. It is my conviction that the world of ideas needed by thoughtful science teachers is much broader than this. The purpose of this book is to enrich the intellectual ecosystem of science teachers as they consider daily how to be a good teacher to all of their students. Because my own work is primarily with new teachers, many of these essays are also about learning to teach science, and how one needs to take competing aims into consideration in order to make decisions in the classroom that lead to the outcomes we want. Occasionally those decisions may involve acts of what U.S. Congressman and civil rights activist John Lewis often calls "good trouble," in which teachers consciously push back against systems and practices that harm students, and challenge long-held institutional or cultural norms that place barriers in the way of students' academic achievement and passion for science.[3]

I spent the first decade of my career as a science teacher in suburban, rural, and urban public-school classrooms, teaching mostly chemistry and physics, along with occasional earth science, biology, or algebra class assignments. Serving twice as a science teacher in the U.S. Peace Corps, first in Kenya and then in Papua New Guinea also gave me a different and more global perspective on science teaching. It also made me rethink my identity and privilege as a white male in teaching subjects that offered access to valued knowledge for students who were often marginalized in schools. Then for the next dozen years, I became involved with university-based science teacher education, where I work today, mostly with students preparing to be secondary science teachers in diverse classrooms. It is no small coincidence that the range of contexts I have experienced in my work informs the central theme of this book: that the main intellectual work of science teachers is figuring out how to make connections between their subject matter and their students. I will argue for the remainder of this book that doing a "good job" as a science teacher requires a thorough knowledge of one's students, a flexible and everdeepening understanding of the science, and a continuing attention to ways in which the science can be made accessible to students so that they might learn it.

★★★

This book is organized into three sections, and the chapters all draw upon real-life science teaching to provide examples of what high quality science teaching looks like. The first section, titled "Student Ideas Are the Raw Material of Our Work," develops the theme that students' prior knowledge ought to be considered a resource rather than an obstacle, and that the intellectual work of good science teaching is thinking about ways to connect the content with what our students bring to learning. Chapter 1 explores the intersection between culturally relevant pedagogy and science teaching through the lens of valuing student ideas. Chapter 2 focuses on the practice of eliciting student ideas so that they may be used productively in the classroom. Chapter 3 is a short but necessary chapter addressing the need for respect and wonder when encountering new student misconceptions. This chapter suggests that when students are sincere about odd ideas, we are being given a gift that will help to teach them. Chapter 4 presents the case study of a teacher, Mr. Teague, who demonstrates what it means to really value students' ideas through the practice of *not* answering his students' questions.

The next section, titled "Real Science, Real Students," addresses the day-to-day issues that occur in science teaching, approached from the perspective of reconsidering the commonplaces of the classroom, such as asking questions, planning, labs, demonstrations, safety, and field trips. Chapter 5 makes a case for the use of essential questions in science class as a way to provide a rationale for units, and connect the science content to real-world issues. Chapter 6 reconsiders the use of laboratory activities, and offers a different view on how science teachers might approach them from the perspective of engaging in model-based inquiry. Chapter 7 continues this discussion about models by examining the role that simulations might play in science learning when they are thought about as models themselves. Chapter 8 takes a fresh look at what safety goggles have to teach us about scientific practices, and Chapter 9 looks at what field trips and guest speakers still have to offer science teachers in an age when their use is becoming increasingly scarce. Chapter 10, which originally appeared in *Rethinking Schools*, tells a story that combines all of the themes in this section, when a field trip to tap maple trees in a city park led to a surprising confession.

In the final section, titled "Science Teacher Learning," the focus is placed on the ways in which novice and veteran science teachers alike improve their teaching practice. Chapter 11 draws upon the legacy of Michael Faraday to create parallels between making observations in science, and learning from watching other teachers teach. Chapter 12 which originally appeared in *Phi Delta Kappan*, deals specifically with the challenges of mentoring student teachers and novice teachers in science classrooms, and offers practical advice for doing so. Chapter 13 is a thought experiment on teacher expertise, situating teacher learning about the practice of differentiating science instruction within the mastery traditions used in martial arts. Chapter 14 concerns the perennial issue of the need for teachers to learn new science, and grapples with the dilemma of deciding what to do about gaps in our knowledge once we have identified them. Chapter 15 moves beyond individual teacher learning to the larger debates about the purposes of school science, and concludes with a closer look at the ways in which real science intersects with the framework of mass public education, examining the tension between school science realists and reformers.

The book ends with a brief and heartfelt plea in the afterword for capable individuals with talents in science to consider science teaching as a career. It is my sincerest hope that this appeal is copied, passed around, and acted upon, because regardless of the reason, our profession is still short-handed and could always use a few more thoughtful science teachers, willing and able to teach real science to real students.

Notes

1 For an extended discussion of this idea, see Popkewitz (1987), and also Cuban (2013).
2 Both The Framework for K-12 Science Education: Practices, Crosscutting Concepts, and Core Ideas (National Research Council, 2012), as well as the Next Generation Science Standards (Achieve Inc., 2013) are important documents for understanding the consensus reached over the past four decades about science education both in the United States and around the world. However, just as the decoding of the human genome led to a new set of problems about understanding the relationship between genome and living organisms, so too does the publication of these standards documents lead to a need to better understand how the desired outcomes of science education are related to the daily work of science teachers. Some believe that if only we have well-designed curricula that reflect these standards, science education will improve. There is truth in this, but I focus my efforts here on a vision of science teachers as autonomous professionals who make continuous decisions for their students' learning, and the curriculum is but one component of this complex job.
3 This is a common refrain from Congressman Lewis, and he has frequently used the phrase as a hashtag (#goodtrouble) on social media (Mettler, 2016). When I was a teacher at Trenton Central High School in New Jersey, one of my physics classes was unexpectedly interrupted by a surprise visit of Congressman Lewis to our school, and I first heard him speak the phrase "good trouble" in telling his life story to our students that day. His recollection of sidestepping the advice from his parents to stay out of trouble is recounted in his book *Walking With the Wind: A Memoir of the Movement* (Lewis & D'Orso, 1999).

PART I

Student Ideas Are the Raw Material of Our Work

1

AIMING FOR CULTURALLY RELEVANT SCIENCE TEACHING

An Argument for Meeting Our Students Where They Are

Raising her hand during a class discussion on genetics, a tenth-grade African American girl in Teresa's eighth-period biology class asked, "Is there a reason that people with darker skin are more inclined to have high blood pressure and things like that?" Having been involved in undergraduate research projects on this topic both in genetics and sociology and earning top grades through all of her courses as an undergraduate, Teresa was readier than most student teachers to answer this question.

Her cooperating teacher, however, was not. This question landed as unwelcome because of the way it interrupted the planned and orderly transfer of information from the teacher, through PowerPoint slides, to the students. "Well, typically in black culture," she began, "they eat a lot of soul food…"

This was more than Teresa could bear. As a Latina—though if pressed she preferred to identify as Dominican—she had experienced this type of racism before, and now felt it even more keenly on behalf of the handful of students of color in this primarily white class. And though it felt risky because of her status as a student teacher, she decided it was necessary to interrupt her cooperating teacher and cause some good trouble.

"Oh my gosh! That's not why!" she said, "Increases in things like high blood pressure are often associated with stress. I have read several studies where it shows that because of the higher incidence of stressors in the lives of minorities, you see strong correlations between highly stressful lives and high blood pressure, and that usually has to do with institutionalized racism, and the possible stresses you'd endure being a minority in this country." She also described to her students the ways in which limited access to supermarkets and fresh food in many minority communities represented another aspect of systemic racism. After a momentary pause—and having nothing further to add—Teresa's cooperating teacher simply continued the genetics lesson.

Teresa told me what happened later, when a few of the students of color had approached her after class. "One of the girls came up," Teresa said, "and she was like, 'That was really cool. Nobody ever talks about *us.*' And she said '*us*' like that."

★★★

In her book, *The Dreamkeepers: Successful Teachers of African American Students*, education researcher Gloria Ladson-Billings identified teachers whose African American students were deemed successful by both the school administration as well as the students' families.[1] Such an assets-based approach turned decades of educational research on its head by looking at what was worthy and good, rather than what was wrong, in the education of black students. In this research, Ladson-Billings looked for commonalities across eight very different teachers, whose classroom practices varied a great deal. With the help of those teachers, she ultimately developed a theory to explain the successful teaching she witnessed, giving it the name *culturally relevant pedagogy.*

A large part of the practice of science—and I include educational research under that umbrella—is the development of models to explain observed phenomena. Models have *explanatory power* to describe how different parts of a system relate to one another, and they also have *predictive power* that can help us reason about what might happen with other inputs or in different circumstances. Consequently, the quality of a model is judged by how well it explains the data, makes predictions, and fits other accepted explanations about the way the world works. Scientists tend to think that a model is on to something when it starts becoming generalizable; offering coherent explanations for other phenomena beyond what it was originally intended to explain. Models are often dynamic, and undergo revisions over time in order to better explain or predict a wider range of observations. Sometimes they are overhauled entirely when anomalous data makes the model no longer plausible. This point is important because it reminds us that models serve the data, and not the other way around.[2]

All of this is to offer a reminder that Ladson-Billings' theory of culturally relevant pedagogy is such an explanatory model, because what her Dreamkeeper teachers had in common was:

- They all had high academic expectations of their students,
- They all offered students regular opportunities to sustain themselves culturally; that is, students were validated in the classroom as cultural individuals, and
- They all sought to develop their students' sociopolitical consciousness so that students could critically analyze the factors that supported social inequalities.

The consequences of understanding the theory of culturally relevant pedagogy lay in its predictive power, with the underlying idea being that when other teachers of African American students engage in these practices, this model predicts their students are more likely to experience success in school.

Teresa's response to her student's question exemplifies all three of these aspects of culturally relevant pedagogy. Rather than witness her students be forced to accept a simplistic and wrong answer, she was prepared to offer a more detailed and sophisticated explanation with deeper connections to the content; which she expected them to understand. And rather than permit the airing of insensitive tropes about black people in a science classroom and allow that action to impact the ways her African American students thought about themselves, Teresa intervened to make sure that her students did not have to accept a caricatured view of themselves and their culture as a price for access to learning about genetics. Finally, Teresa encouraged her students to transform the lifeless knowledge being delivered to them into a tool for understanding and acting on their world. By reframing the issue from an individual matter to a systemic problem, Teresa was raising her students' awareness of the ways in which scientific knowledge matters to human beings organized in society. In a very clear way, Teresa was demonstrating the authentic relationship between scientific knowledge and her students' lives in the world beyond the classroom.

★★★

In my experience, teachers coming into contact with the phrase *culturally relevant teaching* for the first time tend to focus on the root words—culture and relevance—in an effort to make sense of what it might mean for their own pedagogy.

The term *culture* has a common meaning that is often used in reference to the everyday practices—including language, cuisine, and artistic expression—that constitute the ways in which people behave and think. In the field of anthropology, the concept of culture serves as a way to think about the set of rules that guide the habits, behaviors, and norms of a given group of people. From a psychological perspective, culture is the set of perceptual filters that help people interpret the world through an existing framework of understanding.

The slipperiness of the way *culture* is used in everyday speech reflects common misunderstandings about race, ethnicity, and language. All too often, the term is used in the United States and elsewhere as a simplistic proxy to refer to the habits and practices of people who are non-white and non-English-speaking. In this way, some white teachers come to believe that they do not have a culture—only the "other" has cultural practices and beliefs—and that culture is something frozen in time, immutable.[3] Neither is in fact true.

The common way of thinking about *relevance* is in the connection of teaching to something that students are familiar with or care about. One of the reasons we aim for relevance in our teaching is that it serves as a scaffold for learning, providing landmarks for students so that they can recognize where they are. Relevance is valuable, but can be fleeting, especially when rooted in popular culture or if the connection is not particularly strong.

Relevance also relates to issues of childhood growth and developmental appropriateness, and I am reminded of one student teacher in particular who tried very hard to make his teaching relevant for his students.[4] He was quite interested in video games, and as a result many of the examples he used in class at the beginning of the year were drawn from whatever latest game he had played, his idea being that kids loved video games and that mentioning them in conjunction with science would foster their interest. However, his students were in 6th grade in a low-income school, and not only were many of the games targeted at mature adults, they were also simply quite expensive. Instead of providing scaffolds for learning, his examples simply sowed confusion.

Relevance provides students with opportunities to connect new ideas to familiar old ones. When a biology teacher begins a unit on mitosis by asking students to raise their hands if they know someone who has had cancer, he is helping to make explicit connections between subject matter and students' lives. When a physics teacher starts a lesson on Hooke's Law by going around the room and asking where in their lives students have seen springs, she is priming the students to think about all the different places (screen doors, underneath cars, click pens, etc.) where the topic under study intersects with their lives.

In a way, the case for relevance in teaching is really an argument for authenticity, and the removal of barriers to learning. When topics of study are authentic, the degree of relevance to students is immediately apparent. The learning task has an immediate connection to the real world, even more so if it involves accountability to a real audience beyond the classroom. When we choose examples that are familiar to students, we avoid raising roadblocks between their current understandings about the world and what we want them to learn, permitting students to reckon with the science.[5]

★★★

Recall that Ladson-Billings' model of culturally relevant pedagogy states that African American students of teachers who have high academic expectations of their students, regularly offer opportunities for students to sustain themselves as cultural beings, and work on developing their students' sociopolitical consciousness, can reasonably expect to experience success as measured by both their schools and their families. This model has been bolstered now by over two decades of empirical work since it was first published.[6]

When teachers sustain students' cultural identities, it means that students do not have to check their culture at the door as a prerequisite for learning science. Not only that, but teachers who encourage students to be fluent in more than one culture, more than one way of viewing the world, also find opportunities for language and culture to intersect with the content of the lesson.[7] Doing so can also provide an access to the culture of science.

For example, a physics teacher can take time to explore the Spanish word *velocidad* in a lesson on vector and scalar quantities, and help all students think about the differences between *speed* (which just has a magnitude) and *velocity* (which has both magnitude and direction). The Spanish *velocidad* does indeed represent a vector quantity, but has an everyday usage similar to *speed* in English. Spending a short amount of time on this distinction can help students clarify their understanding of physics, as well as helping them to develop conceptual fluency in two languages. Teachers who keep their eyes and ears open for clues about their students' lives outside of school are more likely to identify such teaching moments.[8]

For many teachers, the first step toward sustaining culture is just getting out of the way, and resisting the urge to prevent students from using familiar patterns of communication and engagement, and then leveraging those student resources for deeper learning.[9] I recall a visit to one of my favorite biology classrooms, when the students had aggregated their class data into a table on the whiteboard at the front of the room. I watched as one student took out his phone and snapped a photo of the class data set on the whiteboard. In many schools and classrooms, phones are subject to strict regulation, even as they form the nervous system for adolescent culture at all socioeconomic levels. The teacher in this class had intentionally created a classroom environment in which cell phones were permitted—skirting the edges of school policy—as long as students could justify their use for a scientific purpose. Drawing on both his generational and cultural identities, the student's natural impulse was to use his phone to take a picture of the data, and by encouraging the student to leverage this, the teacher created a space for culture to influence science learning.

Teachers can make these spaces with language as well. As a high school physics and chemistry teacher, I had frequent reasons to count to three, usually for demonstrations when I was about to drop something, switch something on, or light something on fire. Occasionally we might go up to five or six when counting off groups, something we do often in the university classes I now teach. The first time I do this with a class, I typically use Swahili and make my students count: *moja, mbili, tatu* with me. In any given classroom, there can be many different language resources among the students, and if we as teachers leverage these into a cognitively manageable activity like counting, we can get to learn things about our students that we might not otherwise know. I typically try to get students to suggest a language we have not yet used, and there are always surprises beyond the Spanish and French that many students already know; in my classes we have counted in Quichua, Pashto, Bengali, American Sign Language, Portuguese, Ibo, and many other languages. I try to pick a different one each time—and make the whole class say it with me. A student may never have heard their home language in a science classroom before, and my experience is that even this small gesture communicates that they do not have to leave that important piece of who they are at the classroom door as the price of admission for learning science.

***

It also turns out that using relevant and authentic phenomena for investigation helps teachers see a role for their students' cultural resources in science class. Further, when we choose ideas that help develop students' sociopolitical consciousness, we give them an opportunity to critically examine and address issues of justice, fairness, and power—and science no longer seems disconnected from everyday life. For students who experience injustice, unfairness, and powerlessness in their lives, the answer to the question: "When will we ever use this?" is self-evident in these classrooms.

It seems to me that some teachers are overly eager to apply the term "culturally relevant" to their teaching. Similarly, some education researchers and publishers will make claims about the "cultural relevance" of a particular teaching approach, professional development, or set of curricular materials. I often find these claims to be something of a stretch, and wonder if the appropriation of the phrase is primarily for the purposes of self-promotion or out of a desire to be perceived as progressive. This seems especially true when successful outcomes for black students—like the ones whose success was the phenomenon Ladson-Billings set out to explain—are nowhere in sight.

In sharing these ideas—and early drafts of this chapter—with preservice science teachers, one frequent comment was that a teacher like Teresa was more easily able to engage in culturally relevant teaching because of knowledge gained through her own life experiences. Certainly, navigating her own identity growth while making sense of how she was perceived by the dominant culture permitted Teresa to develop an understanding of how harmful stereotypes could be perpetuated in schools.[10] The self-reflective question raised by some preservice teachers in these conversations was: what happens when this is not the case? I found drawing an analogy to learning science content to be convincing in response. Just as a novice might recognize that they need to improve their understanding of biology, chemistry, physics, and earth science in order to be an effective science teacher, so too must teachers who grow up uncritical of the operation of the dominant culture recognize that they have some catching up to do if they are going to be good teachers to all of their students. Admitting one's ignorance, and taking ownership over the responsibility to learn, is a necessary first step.[11]

A teacher like Teresa—fighting to ensure that the science her students learn is less burdened by racism—is not necessarily seeking recognition for enacting culturally relevant pedagogy. Rather, she has internalized its underlying tenets as a consequence of wishing to do right by her students. She has high academic expectations, aims to sustain her students as cultural beings, and works to develop their sociopolitical consciousness not because she is following a formula to be a better teacher, but because she genuinely wants the science taught to her students to be correct and deeply learned. She also sees the laziness of status quo science teaching as actively harmful to students of color and white students alike because of the ways in which knowledge is passed along uncritically. And like the teachers who Ladson-Billings calls *Dreamkeepers*, she takes responsibility for the success of all of the children in her care because she sees her own fate as intertwined with those of her students.

Notes

1 A friend gave me a copy of *The Dreamkeepers* (Ladson-Billings, 1994) just after I had been accepted into graduate school at the University of Wisconsin-Madison, and I was pleasantly surprised to see that the author was a professor there. After I read it, I immediately signed up for her class on Multicultural Perspectives in Education. The class was over-enrolled but she let me in anyway. Shortly thereafter I asked her to be my advisor, and I remain grateful two decades later that she agreed.

2 Models certainly serve to evaluate the validity of new data. As Kuhn (1970) notes however, it is more typical in "normal science" for anomalous data to represent edge cases or faulty measurements rather than signal the start of a scientific revolution in which old models fail and new models are adopted. Morris (2018) thinks Kuhn took

things too far (and had an ashtray thrown at him by Kuhn for telling him as much) because he conflated the models with reality itself.

3 Sleeter's (2001b) discussion of this phenomenon in teacher education explores its impact in detail. In much of her work (Grant & Sleeter, 1985; Sleeter, 1993, 1994, 2001a, 2015), Sleeter suggests strategies for resisting and countering the effects of the dominant culture of whiteness in teaching, curriculum, school structure, educational research, and teacher education, while also recognizing the cultural aspects of whiteness itself.

4 The work of Margaret Beale Spencer (2008) reminds us that even notions of what is "developmentally appropriate" have been tilted towards a conflation of whiteness with normality.

5 The removal of barriers to learning is also a central theme in the Universal Design for Learning curricular framework (Meyer, Rose, & Gordon, 2016).

6 Just to point to one tangible example, Claude Steele's work on stereotype threat (Steele, 2010) investigates the psychological mechanism through which expectations influence academic performance, and he demonstrates how specific positive affirmations of cultural competence serve to mitigate negative effects. There is a clear link here to Ladson-Billings' (1994, 1995, 2006, 2014) work on culturally relevant pedagogy.

7 Banks (1995) terms this the content integration dimension of multicultural education.

8 I am surprised at a how often this idea seems to be interpreted through the lens of essentialism within the everyday discourse of teachers, as if there is one approach for teaching science to Black students, another for Latinx students, etc. My suspicion is that there are cognitive parallels between this sort of flowchart-inspired thinking and the largely discredited folk beliefs about "learning styles" that remain endemic among education professionals (Willingham, Hughes, & Dobolyi, 2015).

9 There is a rich scholarship in science education on this point. See for example: Bang, Warren, Rosebery, & Medin, 2013; B. A. Brown, 2006; B. A. Brown & Spang, 2008; Hudicourt-Barnes, 2003; Warren, Ballenger, Ogonowski, Rosebery, & Hudicourt-Barnes, 2001.

10 This is an example of what Du Bois (1903/1993) called a "double consciousness." It is also a good argument for recruiting more teachers of color into the workforce (Villegas & Davis, 2008).

11 This is the central thesis of Gary Howard's (2006) book, *We Can't Teach What We Don't Know: White Teachers, Multiracial Schools*.

2

ELICITING STUDENTS' IDEAS

Student Ideas as the Raw Material of Science Teachers' Work

None of the students could resist running their hand over the black bear pelt laid out on the table as they took their seats surrounding it. Before Tom could even say hello to the class, people started asking questions about the bear. "Was this caught up here?" one student asked. "What kind of bear is this?" another called out.

Tom, a master environmental educator working at the New Jersey School of Conservation, patiently answered each question, but purposefully did not go into too much detail. He had a question of his own he wanted to ask first. "So," he said addressing the students seated around the bearskin, "What do you know about bears?"

★★★

Good science teaching starts with the premise that student ideas are the raw material of our work. In order to shape those ideas, we need to know what they are. Otherwise our teaching may be transient—like building sand castles or drawing on a sidewalk with chalk—and likely to fade over time, as students revert to ideas that are more familiar and make more sense to them than the science content the teacher intended them to learn. Only when students' ideas are out in the open does it become possible to engage in discussion about the intelligibility, plausibility, or the explanatory power of those ideas.[1]

This does not mean that teachers need to elicit every student's idea about every topic they teach. It can be enough to be aware that for any given science topic, there will be a percentage of students who hold one particular idea, while others will think differently. Even if we cannot predict who exactly will believe what, knowing the possible misconceptions that our students may hold will help us teach them.[2]

There are a range of wonderful strategies for eliciting students' ideas, and plenty of resources to help teachers do that, but here I wish to focus on the question of what we are actually eliciting their ideas about. One kind of elicitation—represented by Tom's question, "What do you know about bears?"—is designed to probe students for the cognitive and cultural resources they bring to the task of learning. In this type of elicitation, there is no need for students to justify their responses; the important thing is to get that prior knowledge out in the open.

When Tom asked, "What do you know about bears?" he knew that most of the students had likely heard quite a bit about bears in their lives. Others, particularly those who had grown up in places where bears were less a part of the culture then they are in the United States, might have less prior knowledge about bears and therefore draw more directly from the bear skin right in front of them. He also knew from years of experience that as students talked, he would hear a number of misconceptions about bears from students, and the conversational tone he used helped to put the students at ease because they were not being judged on the correctness of each idea.

Elicitations take stock of students' cognitive and cultural resources, and help teachers plan for instruction. A prompt for elicitations may take the form of an open-ended question that can be answered with a range of divergent responses. Examples include:

- "What are some reasons why we might look at things under a microscope?"
- "Where have you seen something made from rock in your everyday life?"
- "What are some situations where water might change from one phase to another?"

Such questions have multiple possible answers, and students' responses inform teachers about the existing resources that students can bring to bear on a further understanding of the topic. The best-designed prompts allow for every student to give an answer and participate in the discussion. This type of elicitation has its limits, however. In the examples above, students would need to have familiarity with microscopes, rocks, ice, and steam. If Tom had asked a group of first-graders, "Tell me what you already know about woolly adelgids," he might not have unearthed too many cognitive and cultural resources.[3]

I have had conversations with teachers who are skeptical about the whole notion of eliciting student ideas, and their argument goes something like this: if I am going to teach DNA transcription and translation to my biology students, it may be a topic that is brand new to them. In fact, their understanding about DNA may be so limited that if I ask them what ideas they have about transcription and translation, they are not going to have any because they have never even thought about those things before.

I would actually agree that it makes little sense to ask students at the beginning of such a unit, "What do you know about DNA transcription and translation?" There are many times when I have seen teachers engage in this type of elicitation at the beginning of a unit or lesson, and it almost always ends up positioning students as ignorant, as if they should already know.[4] The problem in such a case is that teachers are attempting to elicit prior knowledge about scientific *concepts* instead of tapping into students' ideas about a *phenomenon*. The distinction is subtle but important. Asking students about a concept they have never encountered before can be confusing for them. However, if you show them a phenomenon that requires crafting an explanation of some sort, even if it is simple, students can immediately begin by drawing on what they know and from what they have observed about the puzzling phenomenon.

★★★

Imari cued up the video clip and got the attention of her high school biology class. "I'm going to play you a short segment from a documentary that has a mystery for you to think about," she said to her students. She pressed play and the video showed multiple clownfish brushing up against a sea anemone. The narrator on the video described how sea anemones use their stinging tentacles to paralyze, ensnare, and consume small fish. But clownfish, he continued, seemed to use the anemone's tentacles for protection from other predators.

"How can this be?" asked the narrator, at which point Imari stopped the video. She turned on the lights and said, "I'd like for you to get into your groups and come up with as many possible ideas as you can for that question. Give each idea its own sticky note. How might it be possible for a fish to live so close to another organism that is so dangerous?"

★★★

A second kind of elicitation is illustrated by Imari's prompt to her students about the puzzle posed in the video, which allowed students to share their ideas even if they had never seen or heard about clownfish or sea anemones before watching the video.[5] In this elicitation, students were presented with a puzzling phenomenon and tasked with describing their ideas about how the unseen processes operate. Such an elicitation takes advantage of the human capacity for generating inferences and explanations.

For example, if I walk into a room, notice a burning smell and see a blackened popcorn bag next to a microwave oven, I can put together a fairly plausible explanation of what happened before I got there. The problem with elicitation prompts that are only about concepts is that they do not provide students the opportunity to create explanations. Imagine how different this lesson would have looked if Imari began by asking, "What do you know about mutualism?"

Eliciting students' ideas about a puzzling phenomenon offers an opportunity to explore the big ideas in the science curriculum in ways that are accessible and familiar to students. This is where the teacher's knowledge of students becomes critical, because by being familiar with both the students and the content, the teacher will be able to pick the phenomena that resonate with their students.

When we present students with a puzzling phenomenon, what we are really doing is giving them both an opportunity to draw upon their existing resources and put them together in a way that makes sense to them. For example, if we present students with a hot and a cold beaker of water, and put a drop of food coloring in each, the phenomenon is that the beaker with the hot water disperses the color much more rapidly than the beaker with the cold water. The elicitation question we might put to students in a case like this is: what ideas do you have about why the color spreads more rapidly in the hot water? In order to respond, students must draw upon whatever existing knowledge they have in order to construct an explanation. They may draw on their life experiences—like making juice from a mix or dropping tints into a bathtub—as analogies for their explanations. And even if the student gives a perfect textbook answer that reflects a sophisticated knowledge of kinetic theory, they can still be pointed towards other components of the phenomenon (like the downward trajectory of the food coloring drop) that still require explanation.

Phenomena can be videos, demonstrations, or even just simple descriptions of situations. Often, they describe events that unfold over time, and usually entail an unseen process in some way.[6] Students may not be able to explain the whole phenomenon, but often they are able to bring in ideas that hold the prospect of being part of an explanation. Even something completely foreign to students, like observing the slow fall of a strong magnet through a copper tube, can be the source for student ideas. A teacher who asks students for ideas to explain the behavior of the magnet—rather than asking, "Who remembers what Lenz's law is?"—will get much greater participation on the part of students, and also get everyone thinking.[7]

Prompts for elicitation can also be genuine questions that result from everyday experiences in the classroom. I was recently in one chemistry class where students reacted solid magnesium with hydrochloric acid, and then heated the resulting liquid until only a white solid remained. The class ran out of time and left the white solid in the evaporating dishes, and when they came back the next day they found that overnight the white solid had turned into a puddle of liquid. This was a good puzzling phenomenon, albeit one only tangentially related to the lesson on empirical formulas the teacher had planned for that day, and the teacher—abandoning the "do-now" he had previously planned for the first five minutes of class—made good use of the unexpected situation with a class discussion.

Science teachers who start keeping their eyes open for puzzling phenomena will begin seeing them everywhere. Recently in a grocery store in Colorado, my family and I noticed that all of the bags in the snack aisle seemed to be filled with a little extra air, making them more puffed out than they are in New Jersey. We bought a few bags for our ride through Rocky Mountain National Park, and later when we stopped the car at the alpine tundra, one small bag of popcorn on the center console resembled a balloon; there was not a single wrinkle or indentation in the bag. The signs told us that we were at 12,000 feet, about a mile higher in elevation than we had been in town. I took out my phone and began to record video of the swollen popcorn bag. It would make a great puzzling phenomenon.

Notes

1 This language comes directly from foundational work on teaching science for conceptual change (Hewson, Beeth, & Thorley, 1998; Posner, Strike, Hewson, & Gertzog, 1982; Strike & Posner, 1992), which informs this chapter greatly.

2   The MOSART project report (P. M. Sadler, Sonnert, Coyle, Cook-Smith, & Miller, 2013) makes the case that the ability to identify common student misconceptions is a valid measure of science teacher quality.

3   The wooly adelgid is an invasive species of aphid that has become a major killer of the hemlock tree population over the past decade in New Jersey and the northeastern United States. It is currently being fought with some success through the introduction of a predator beetle, Sasajiscymnus tsugae (Eschtruth, Evans, & Battles, 2013). I learned this at the New Jersey School of Conservation.

4   This can be worse if there are one or more students who do know, because it sends a message of academic exclusion to others.

5   Many students in the class immediately made a connection to the opening scene of the Pixar animated movie, Finding Nemo, in which a clownfish uses a sea anemone for protection from a predator.

6   Windschitl, Thompson, & Braaten (2008) developed a set of tools for teachers to use in the identification and development of phenomena appropriate for model-based inquiry, and note that good phenomena or "anchoring events" for classroom use have comprehensible causal underpinnings, (p. 16). See chapter 2 of Windschitl, Thompson, and Braaten (2018) for more detail on identifying big science ideas, selecting anchoring events and meaningful essential questions, and sequencing learning activities.

7   At the end of a summer working with teachers in Tanzania, I was sitting around a fire talking with a mix of Americans and locals, when one young Tanzanian man asked me what I taught in America. When I answered that I was a physics teacher, he stood up and said in a fast monotone voice: "A current induced in a circuit due to a change in a magnetic field is so directed as to oppose the change in flux and to exert a mechanical force opposing the motion!" He had just recited Lenz's Law. "I have no idea what I just said," he laughed with an undercurrent of resentment, "but it got me an A in physics." I think of him often whenever I am made aware of students who earn good grades without enjoying or even understanding the ideas of the science.

3

EVERY MISCONCEPTION A SHINY PEBBLE

Glimpsing Beautiful and Productive Extensions of Prior Knowledge

Donna moved among her students as they cut out the photocopied chromosomes from the handout. Unbeknownst to the students, there were 47 chromosomes, instead of the more typical 46 for humans, and when students made matched pairs, they would find an extra chromosome, do a little research in their packets, and recognize that the karyotype was indicative of a person with Down's Syndrome. It was an activity that Donna's cooperating teacher used every year during the genetics unit, and she was glad to see her high school students engaged in the lesson. She knelt down next to one group who was having a little trouble matching the chromosome pairs, and she drew their attention to the patterns of light and dark bands. "The size is more important than the shape," she said, "and look at the alleles." She pointed to the light and dark bands along the length of each chromosome shape on the photocopied handout. Of course, it was not scientifically accurate, but was an idea I had not heard before, and I was captivated.[1]

Every misconception I encounter is like a shiny pebble on the beach. I love looking at them, rolling them around, and trying to figure out where they came from. Donna's was not difficult to figure out, nearly every biology textbook has an illustration of a length of DNA highlighted on a chromosome to represent a gene, and Donna—even as a biology major in college—likely took that representation and interpreted the dark bands of densely-packed chromatin on the chromosome as exactly such a band. Further, she likely applied her knowledge of genetics in calling it an allele instead of a gene because she knew that in a chromosome pair, the gene might be coded slightly differently on each.[2]

This sort of forensic analysis of misconceptions is second nature to master teachers because in the process of unraveling the mystery of an idea's source, paths leading toward future understanding are also revealed. In Donna's case, this could be as simple as providing images of chromosomes under higher magnification, to show that the light and dark bands are a function of the coiling of the DNA. Donna could also be pressed to investigate how scientists know where genes begin and end, and whether that information can be visually ascertained at all. To an attentive observer, Donna's use of the word "allele" as a label is a key to understanding her whole cognitive architecture around the topic of genetics.

This is why I find it incredibly frustrating whenever I hear mockery of students' misconceptions, which happens a great deal more frequently in private teacher conversations than one might hope. When a student is sincere to us about an idea that seems absurd, we are being handed a map of their brain.[3] A teacher who interprets sense-making as stupidity is committing educational malpractice.

Sitting in the back of science rooms, I often get to hear the most wonderful misconceptions. One of my favorites happened in the back of a physics room, during a lesson on sounds and waves. Students were given the task of answering a series of questions from the board, and then constructing a concept map using a list of vocabulary words. They were permitted to work together, and one pair of students began to debate the meaning of the word *mute*. One student claimed that mute was a type of sound, while another said that it meant the same as quiet. It was not hard to envision the student's idea of a television remote broadcasting one type of sound wave that canceled out others. They each ended up making their concept maps their own way, but even that brief exchange gave me insight into how each of them was thinking about the nature of sound.

Sometimes misconceptions take a while to bubble to the surface. In one classroom where students were developing models on flip-chart paper to explain the dispersion of food dye in water, an interesting argument emerged between two groups of students. One faction felt that when the beaker of water turned a uniform color, the particles of dye and the water molecules were evenly mixed, as their model demonstrated with red (dye) and blue (water) dots evenly distributed. However, the other part of the class felt that because food dye changed the color of things, it had actually changed the color of the water molecules themselves. I think about how my own high school chemistry teachers might have handled this, and it is difficult to think about any response that would not contain some level of sarcasm or derision directed at the students for believing such a thing. There is a misconception among some teachers that giving voice to a wrong idea in a classroom is harmful, as if it could spread like an airborne infection. Decades of cognitive and educational research have shown these fears to be unfounded.[4]

In this case, the teacher not only permitted a student-to-student discussion to occur in class, but also made sure to facilitate it in a way that gave each group an opportunity to question one another in a manner that furthered the conversation. When pressed by peers to explain whether or not they also thought that the dye was made of atoms and molecules, the color-change group seemed to give ground and admit that they had not quite thought of that. When conversations like these—in which the comparison of science ideas happens in the open spaces of the classroom instead of remaining closed away in the private recesses of students' minds—occur regularly in every classroom, those of us working to reform science teaching will know that we have made real progress.

Notes

1 It is reasonable to ask if misusing a vocabulary word or scientific term ought to be considered evidence that someone holds a misconception about an important scientific idea. This question quickly leads to Wittgensteinian debates about the relationships between ideas and language, but it does seem reasonable to concede that a misused word need not represent a misconception (Hofstadter & Sander, 2013). However, it may be a clue that a person's understanding of a central scientific idea or concept may not be aligned with that of the broader scientific community. For example, when someone refers to a warm winter day as "global warming," they are using a phrase that more properly refers to the measured fraction-of-a-degree annual average rise in global temperature, and serves as an indicator of the way that the person has organized their knowledge about climate change more generally.

2 It was a wonderful example of "faulty extensions of productive prior knowledge," to use the phrase coined by Smith, diSessa, and Roschelle, (1993, p. 152).

3 When I was seven and infatuated with all things dinosaur-related, I was genuinely convinced that all pebbles were fossilized dinosaur poop. The idea made total sense to me.

4 See Larkin (2012) for an extended discussion of this point.

4

RESPONDING TO STUDENT QUESTIONS WITHOUT GIVING ANSWERS

"Maybe it Will Just Have to Remain a Mystery Forever"

The assertion of ignorance is a pedagogical strategy that dates back to the earliest accounts of teaching, and is probably even older than that.[1] When the responsibility for responding to an inquiry is redirected back onto the student, it sends a message that the struggle to think through the question is more important than the answer itself. Educators have long known that it is more likely for students to recall answers they have previously figured out on their own, compared with something they were simply told. However, like many aspects of teaching, being able to do something as seemingly simple as *not* answering a question from a student turns out to be surprisingly difficult.

This is especially true for science teachers, many of whom have spent countless hours mastering their own understandings and are eager to share their hard-won knowledge, especially when doing so comes with admiration, relief, and gratitude from students. Not answering questions may take even more skill than answering them, and when my own pre-service science teachers ask me how to not answer their students' questions, I usually tell them about Mr. Teague.

★★★

I first met Mr. Teague many years ago when I was working as a substitute for another physics teacher with whom he shared a room, and I was immediately struck by the way he did not answer his students' questions. Much later, when I asked if I might spend a little time watching him teach, he jumped at the opportunity, saying that having an education researcher in his classroom meant that he might also be able to learn something. I started coming by weekly, and brought doughnuts, which Mr. Teague always shared with his homeroom students and the other science teachers.[2]

Mr. Teague's physics classroom was located on the top floor of his school, at the distant end of a long hallway far from the buzz of activity in the rest of the building. It was not a classroom anyone had to pass on their way to somewhere else, and this contributed to an atmosphere of safety and isolation; an oasis of tranquility in a bustling urban school.[3] His classroom was one in which students were invited to act like scientists themselves, and there was usually some sort of equipment out on the back tables, as well as a demonstration apparatus up front that the students were encouraged to play around with at their leisure. An enormous slide rule hung by pulleys above the front chalkboard, and a bookshelf of popular physics books sat in front of the teacher desk. Cabinets overflowing with force tables, oscilloscopes, wave tanks, and old computers took up the side wall, and low-set black lab benches filled the back third of the room.

Each time I visited Mr. Teague's classroom, it seemed that he was teaching differently. On days when students were involved in an ongoing lab, he would give them the bare minimum of instructions before sending them back to the lab tables. When starting a new topic, he would show the students video clips, which he stopped frequently to add commentary. There were also days when he lectured and performed physics demonstrations for the students. Students in the class kept a lab book on quadrille paper in which they also recorded class notes. Mr. Teague would examine and mark these after each lab activity, yet the huge pyramid of books to mark on his side table never seemed to decrease in size. While in many respects, it resembled a typical physics classroom, Mr. Teague's class was much different than my own experience as a student in high-school physics.

While my own physics teacher in high school had certainly worked hard to foster a love of physics in his students, I often felt as if physics was a disconnected series of facts to be memorized. Even in lab, when the opportunity of discovery is greatest, it often felt as if I were working toward some predetermined goal. The most potent symbol of this type of learning is the "percent error" statistic. By the use of a simple formula, a student is able to determine how far away their results are from an "actual" value. The hidden message in such classrooms that there is a "right" answer, and the authority of finding it lies beyond the student.[4]

One mark of a healthy classroom environment is the presence of a substantial amount of subject-related talking by students. Asking questions, to the teacher and to the other students, is an important part of this discourse, and in my visits, there were certainly lots of questions asked in Mr. Teague's class. These ranged from simple questions about requesting supplies and clarifying laboratory procedure to more complex questions about what would happen if someone traveling at the speed of light threw a ball. When I first saw Mr. Teague's teaching in action, I noticed that sometimes he answered students' questions quite thoroughly, while other times he hardly answered them at all.

What I discovered was that Mr. Teague's responses to his students' questions depended on both the type of information being requested, and the urgency with which he thought the possession of an answer was necessary. Over time I was able to identify five different types of responses, and when I shared my analysis with him, Mr. Teague added a sixth that I had missed, one which was much more difficult to observe. Looking across each of these types of responses below, it is evident that deciding whether it was more important for students to engage in productive struggle or to have an answer was almost always in the forefront of Mr. Teague's decision-making about responding to his students' questions.

Playful Non-answers / "I don't know"

These answers were mostly given in response to the "is this right?" variety of questioning. Mr. Teague affectionately referred to this category of answer as "creative sarcasm," but it was clearly more than that. Each time that Mr. Teague answered a question in this way, he saw it as a conscious choice to foster an understanding of the nature of science on the part of his students. "This way," Mr. Teague says, "nature is the arbiter. Nature, or the equipment, is the bad guy. The teacher isn't the one giving the bad news, it's the data."

STUDENT: (*hooking up a circuit*) Am I doing it right?

TEACHER: You're doing it right if it works. You're not doing it right if it doesn't work.

STUDENT: (*student working on computer circuit simulation*) Is this relationship inverse-squared or just inverse?

TEACHER: It could be inverse, or inverse-squared, or maybe it'll just have to remain a mystery forever.

STUDENT: (*showing Mr. Teague the lab setup with hands on the two different power supplies*) If I keep this one constant and keep increasing this one, will this [ammeter reading] increase too?

TEACHER: (*smiling*) Well, it'll either increase or it won't.

Clarifying Questions/Reflective Statements

For these, Mr. Teague tended to sidestep answering the actual question and instead focused on making the student feel like they themselves had the authority to provide an answer based on their experiences in the class. He did this with simple statements that reflected what the student had already done or already knew. Sometimes Mr. Teague chose pointed questions in order to force students to make the conceptual connections needed to answer their own questions.

STUDENT: (*pointing to a component of the current balance*) Do we measure the length from here to here or from there to there?

TEACHER: The electricity comes in here, and goes along like this (*traces path with finger*).

STUDENT: Oh, so we measure this whole thing.

STUDENT: (*gesturing towards the graph on the computer screen*) Is this destructive [interference]?

TEACHER: Well, it says "totally destructive" [on the instruction sheet] doesn't it? And it looks like you still have a wave at this point.

STUDENT: (*pointing at their circuit setup*) This looks right, but I just want to be sure.

TEACHER: Well, you hooked this up here, and I see the wires connected there and there.

This type of response allowed the students to see their particular questions from a different perspective, and this usually had a clarifying effect that permitted students to answer their own questions by themselves.

Procedurally Suggestive

While still forcing the student to engage in the intellectual challenge of the activity, there was an element of practicality to these responses as well, as they contained more of a hint on how to proceed than the previous categories. By responding this way, Mr. Teague attempted to assist the student without giving away too much or vesting too much authority in the science teacher as a sole source of answers.

STUDENT: (*showing Mr. Teague a piece of apparatus*) Our L-clips aren't working.

TEACHER: (*wiggles a loose L-clip*) You can play with them a bit. (*walks away*)

STUDENT: (*referring to a circuit breaker reset button on the power supply*) Can you come over and tell us if this button is popped out?

TEACHER: I'll bet your ammeter will do that for you.

STUDENT: That's what we're trying to test.

TEACHER: Oh, so *both* ammeters are broken?

STUDENT: Yeah, it...Oh, it must be the wire.

STUDENT: (*showing Mr. Teague her data*) Is this right?

TEACHER: I don't know. We'll have to see when we look at this (*points to the sample graph on the board*) and see how it fits.

STUDENT: (*hooking up a circuit*) How do you know if the current is flowing the right way?

TEACHER: Some people think about positive and negative. Some people just hook it up and see if it goes the direction they want.

Direct Answers in Pursuit of a Larger Question

Direct answers to questions that arose in the course of an inquiry-based activity were offered less frequently than other types of responses, but appeared to be necessary on occasion in order to move a student along towards more substantial questions. They were the answers of last resort for the big questions, but occasionally time constraints made their use pragmatic.

"It's very much a function of how rushed I feel and the level of stress," Mr. Teague told me. "Sometimes I know they're just going to ask a friend. Sometimes I want that and sometimes I don't. Usually what happens if they don't get it, they'll come in during lunch or after school and I'll clue them in much more. If it's a summary thing, I run the risk that if I don't tell them they'll never get it."

"And if you do, they still might not," I added.

"Exactly," he said.

STUDENT: (*obviously frustrated trying to take a measurement on a current balance that will not stop moving—looks to Mr. Teague and effectively communicates her question nonverbally*).

TEACHER: That's the hardest part of this lab. There's parallax and sometimes it keeps moving up and down. It's okay to sort of stop it in the middle.

STUDENT: (*showing Mr. Teague her setup*) Does this go here?

TEACHER: If I said no, you would not know too much more, would you? So I'll say no.

STUDENT: (*talking to Mr. Teague with entire lab group. They are uncomfortable with the data they have collected*) Can we do this over?

TEACHER: Sure. The equipment's over there (*students begin to walk away*). Can I see your data? (*One student hands Mr. Teague her lab notebook and he looks it over*). Actually your data is good enough to start analyzing, you don't have to do it over.

STUDENT: For the beats, do you want us to draw all three of these [peaks on the curve]?

TEACHER: Yes. It's complicated I know. Actually it is hard to draw so it's okay if you just pick two sections [of the graph] and draw all the beats.

Administrative or Safety-oriented Direct Answers

It might seem unnecessary to include this category, but the fact that Mr. Teague answered these administrative or safety-oriented questions in a "regular" way, allowed the students to see that Mr. Teague was not opposed to answering all of the questions that were posed to him.

STUDENT: Is this circuit setup okay?

TEACHER: Why don't you turn that [power supply] down, I think it's about to blow.

STUDENT: Do you have some clear tape?

TEACHER: Not much. Here (*hands the student a roll of masking tape, which works fine*).

TEACHER: Is everything working okay?

STUDENT: Is it okay if we leave it [the power supply] plugged in?

TEACHER: Sure.

Questions Unasked and Unanswered

Mr. Teague himself added the sixth category, after he agreed that the other five categories were an accurate reflection of his practice. There were times, he told me, when he made a conscious decision *not* to make himself available for questioning. This was easily accomplished by going out in the hall, tinkering with something in the prep room, or by simply staying in the front of the room and out of the lab area. Without his presence as a resource, his intent was to force students to solve problems on their own.

"Though I don't want them just sitting there," he told me. "If they're not asking each other any questions, then I'll have some to ask." While he still monitored students' conversations as they worked, by choosing carefully which times to make himself physically unavailable for questioning, he intentionally forced his students to rely on each other for figuring things out.

★★★

During my time in his classroom, I found that his students realized that they could put *me* to the test of whether or not I understood the way Mr. Teague responded to their questions. Because Mr. Teague had introduced me to his classes as a fellow physics teacher, I was regularly asked questions by the students if I happened to be standing in the right place at the right time.

One morning, I was watching a group of students struggle with a circuit containing a few bulbs, an ammeter, and a power supply. The bulbs were lighting, but they were getting no reading on the ammeter. It was evident to me that they had their positive and negative terminals on the ammeter switched, because whenever they closed the circuit I could see the needle moving ever so slightly to the left of zero, a sign that the current was moving in the opposite direction. Finally, in frustration, one of the students turned to me and said, "How come nothing's happening when we turn the power on?" I decided to try and answer this question the way I thought Mr. Teague might.

"Do it again, let me see," I said.

"Look. Nothing's happening," the student asserted.

I watched the needle drift the millimeter or so back to zero. I decided on a response midway between clarifying and procedurally suggestive. "*Something* is happening," I said and left it at that. The group scratched their heads for a little bit longer but eventually figured it out after I had walked away.

It would have been very easy for me to simply tell them which wires were hooked up backwards, but this would have had two drawbacks. In the short term, the students would have been robbed of the opportunity to think through and solve a problem of their own creation. In the long term, it would have reinforced the notion that physics teachers, and not students themselves, are the only authoritative sources for knowledge in the classroom. This seemed consistent with Mr. Teague's view of teaching, and when I shared this story with him, he agreed that I had treated this situation much in the same way he would have.

"What's funny sometimes," he said, "is that the kids who are dependent on the teacher for answers get really frustrated in my class. A few years back there were these two kids…one of them ended up dragging me down into a meeting with the principal, it was the cutest thing actually, and she said to him, 'This guy is not doing his job.' Now she's a friend and she's come around, and sees why I do that. I've actually developed a little bit of a reputation in the school, and now even the biology and chemistry teachers will tell their students: 'You know, when you get to physics, the teacher isn't going to answer a question like that so you might as well get used to figuring it out on your own now.'"

A Copenhagen Interpretation

On the wall in the back of Mr. Teague's classroom is a famous picture of the 1928 Copenhagen gathering of physicists, and next to it is an enormous periodic table published around the same time, which Mr. Teague told his classes was the first one ever purchased by the school. Numerous squares on the table were blank, because at the time some of the elements we know about today had not yet been discovered. He told me that the reason he likes to keep the poster up is to remind his students that all of what they study in his Introductory Physics class—which includes mechanics, optics, sound, electricity, and magnetism— only takes them through what was known in physics up until the early 20th century. It is a powerful reminder that what we now know has not always been known, and that much of our current knowledge has blank squares of its own.

This periodic table with the blank spaces in it is also a metaphor for the way Mr. Teague views how people learn to pose and solve problems. The scientists who eventually filled in the missing elements on the periodic table did not do so by appealing to an authority for answers; they did it by asking questions, posing problems, and designing and carrying out their own investigations. Of course, students have numerous resources to help them find answers, such as friends, textbooks, and the Internet, but that is also the point. Scientists do not work alone, they are part of a scientific community, and as students learn how to operate within this community they become better scientific thinkers, working much like scientists do outside of schools.

By viewing student questions as integral components of learning how to pose and solve problems, rather than as ends in themselves, Mr. Teague was also teaching his students how to think and act like scientists. In science, crafting good questions to ask is often even more important than the answers. When Mr. Teague said, "Maybe it'll just have to remain a mystery forever," he meant it, because scientists must contend with the ever-present possibility that the answers they seek will remain elusive. While evidence may never provide perfect answers to our students' questions, it will almost certainly help them in deciding what question to ask next, as well as empowering them to feel that they have the authority to do the asking.

Notes

1 My personal favorite historical example is the way that Socrates baits Euthyphro with his plea: "…I am anxious to become your pupil… I appeal to you to tell me what you were insisting just now that you definitely know: what you mean by piety and impiety." (Plato, Tredennick, & Tarrant, 1993, p. 24). As a new teacher, I had heard about "the Socratic method" of teaching, but no matter what educational books I read, I could never quite get a handle on exactly what that was. Then I hit upon the strategy of simply reading Plato's direct accounts of Socrates' dialogues, and the idea finally made sense. I now hold an imaginary scene of Socrates in my mind, in earnest appeal before a group of modern-day teachers, "Explain to me what the characteristic of this Socratic method is in itself, so that by fixing my eyes upon it and using it as a pattern, I may be able to describe any teaching—yours or anyone else's—as Socratic if it corresponds to the pattern and non-Socratic if it does not."

2 I had received an inside tip from another staff member that this was a good idea. It was.

3 As a teacher, my own physics classroom was usually similarly situated, and I have seen many schools where this is also the case. This suggests that the opposite may have been true, and the design was to ensure that the rest of the school was isolated safely away from us. Physics classrooms can be noisy places.

4 The science education literature refers to the idea of establishing an authority for assessing knowledge claims as "epistemic agency" (Fricker, 2007; E. Miller, Manz, Russ, Stroupe, & Berland, 2018).

PART II

Real Science, Real Students

5

HELA CELLS, HIGH-SPEED CHASES, AND OTHER ESSENTIAL QUESTIONS

Because Science Class Should Not Be a Trivia Game

The only sound in the biology classroom was the voice of one student as he began reading aloud: "On 4 October 1951, a young black woman named Henrietta Lacks died of cervical cancer…" An image of the book cover for *The Immortal Life of Henrietta Lacks* was projected on the front screen as he read.[1] At the end of each paragraph, Grace called on a different student to continue. This was not a strategy she used often—after all, the students had been assigned the article to read for homework—but the hushed and respectful tone she set for the read-aloud was necessary for the subsequent conversation she had planned. Some students tried to break into the reading with questions, but Grace held them at bay. Students heard that HeLa cells, which are commonly used in research because of their unique properties, were named after <u>H</u>enrietta <u>L</u>acks, the patient from whom they were harvested without consent. "Yet," another reader continued, "Henrietta's body lies in an unmarked grave, while her children have revealed they did not learn for more than 20 years that their mother's cells were still alive and had been used to create an entire branch of medical science."[2] Grace asked the students to discuss at their tables whatever thoughts they had about what they had just heard.

Once they had talked for a bit, she quieted the class and asked, "So how are you feeling about this?" The students' responses covered a wide range of topics, from health insurance and the purpose of hospitals, to what it means to sign a form and give consent. One student commented that race had to be a factor in the story of HeLa cells, and another thought that it was unfair that the family received nothing from the research. "So," Grace asked, setting the table with an essential question that would guide the next week of mitosis lessons, "who do you think owns the rights to their cells?"

★★★

Typically, essential questions are open-ended, without a single definitive answer, and require students to synthesize information across a range of sources and perspectives as they progress through a topic. A well-written essential question serves as a portal to the discipline, in that being able to address the question represents mastery of the intended learning subject matter.[3] The driving purpose of an essential question is to kindle a student's internal motivation for a topic by situating the subject matter to be learned within an authentic context, and effective essential questions are designed to ensure that student learning is propelled by important and recurring themes.

When science teachers use essential questions to frame their units, they provide students with another pathway for learning the science content. Sometimes essential questions press for an explanation to a puzzling phenomenon, like, "Why does the moon seem to change its shape?" Others create openings for the science to connect to a broad range of social issues, and ask students to develop value judgments.

The ethical and moral dilemmas we face as a society often emerge naturally in a science classroom within certain topics. Studying the atom may precipitate discussions about nuclear energy and weapons. A unit on genetics may lead to a dialogue about the ethics of stem cell research or the use of genetically modified organisms in the food supply. A lesson on hurricanes and severe weather may serve as a stepping stone to a debate about segregated housing patterns and construction in flood-prone areas. Science education often makes space for discussion, debate, and dialogue about such issues, and while some are considered dispassionately at a distance ("Should humans colonize Mars?"), others are immediate and visceral ("Why do so many students in our school have asthma?").[4]

There are a number of different ways for essential questions to draw upon authentic problems to frame science learning. One is the notion that science class is an appropriate place to discuss and debate *socio-scientific issues* of importance.[5] Socio-scientific issues are more than just discussions with opinions; they are arguments informed by scientific reasoning and evidence. Their use in science classes can be seen as a way to enact sophisticated educational objectives of evaluation, and as a justification for learning particular content. For example, the socio-scientific issue of whether or not humans ought to tinker with the DNA of sex cells or an embryo in order to produce a "designer baby," provides a compelling rationale for students to learn about genetics and meiosis.

Another use for essential questions is in *problem-based learning* approaches to teaching science, where the essential question is framed as a problem in need of a solution. Though there is as yet no consensus on the essential features of problem-based learning, one obvious element they all share is that student learning is oriented toward the development of a solution to a particular problem, with teachers serving as a resource as needed.[6] Even though this approach is often quite group-based, one recent empirical study suggested that effective problem-based learning resulted from "engagement with contextualized problems" more so than social factors arising from collaboration.[7] This suggests that the choice of a good essential question has important consequences for student learning.

One other function played by essential questions involves *justice-centered* approaches to science teaching—sometimes called teaching science for social justice—that comes from a more critical tradition, which positions individual learners as actors engaged in a struggle for a more just society and human freedom.[8] This justice-centered approach to science teaching includes paying attention to how students can question assumptions and participate in ways that communicate their work products to a wider audience, a component that aligns well with current conceptions of scientific practice. In Grace's class, students invoked notions of justice in asking whether Henrietta Lacks' cells would have been taken if she had been a white man, raising questions about race, gender, and the generation of scientific knowledge. As a class primarily comprised of students of color, this was not a theoretical concern.

★★★

Here are some examples of good essential questions I have encountered over the past decade working with teachers in science classes:

- What is the effect of hunting on the deer population in Wisconsin?
- When I shut off the light, what happens to the electrons in the wire?
- Should human cloning be allowed?
- How does a cell membrane "know" what to let pass?
- What counts as climate change?
- What is the impact of the nearby coal plant on the health of the people in the neighborhood?[9]
- How does radiation both cause and cure cancer?[10]

Some essential questions are robust and perennial, and can be used across multiple contexts and even grade levels. Others are more local and short-lived, particular to a time and place, and come carefully crafted from teachers who have studied their students' lives and school communities for connections to the subject matter.

For example, one year when I was teaching physics, tragedy hit the community when a police car killed an elderly pedestrian during a high-speed chase very near to the school. In the aftermath, a comment in the newspaper posed by a local resident struck me as a great essential question for the unit we were about to start on work and energy: should high-speed car chases be legal? When I raised this question with my class, there was great interest, and though many students wanted to debate the legal dimensions of the question, I made room for the discussion because I had learned to recognize the importance of catching a wave of interest when one rolls in. Over the next month, as I taught a unit on work, energy, and the conservation laws, I would raise the police chase question every once in a while, adding to the physics at the heart of the question about when a chase was safe versus when it was unsafe. The big science idea concerned the relationship between an object's velocity and its kinetic energy, and how doubling the car's speed during a high-speed pursuit would quadruple the damage it could cause in a collision.[11] Students had a chance to summarize their thinking about it in an end-of-unit essay, which confirmed for me that the essential question had served its purpose well.

A good essential question accomplishes multiple ends. First, it provides students with a genuine problem, one whose answer is not apparent or easily discovered with an Internet search, and encourages students' interest as a result. Second, an essential question connects to a big idea in science, even if it is not immediately obvious. Perhaps the most important function played by an essential question is that it serves as a touchstone to which the class returns as students progress through a unit. An essential question can be an explicit and ever-present part of the curriculum, but it can also be a filament of a theme that binds fragments of topics together and prevents science class from turning into a trivia game.

Like the question Grace raised with her class about what it even means to have rights over one's own cells, the richest essential questions are the ones that have complex roots in the underlying disciplinary science, have implications for both teachers and students alike, and raise new questions as they are revisited over time. In Grace's class, these deeper questions emerged as students studied DNA, heredity and mitosis. Was Henrietta Lacks herself still alive in those cells somehow? What does it actually mean for something—or someone—to be alive? While such questions may prove resistant to easy answers, they undoubtedly kindle the fires of inquiry in the minds of students who, when provided with the scientific knowledge and tools by their teachers, continue to stoke them ever brighter.

Notes

1 Skloot, 2010.
2 The reading that Grace assigned her class to read was abstracted from a longer newspaper article (McKie, 2010) about Skloot's book.
3 Though it is possible to look at the curriculum theory scholarship of Herbert Spencer, John Dewey, and Joseph Schwab as foundational to the conceptualization of "essential questions," the modern day incarnation owes a debt to the Coalition for Essential Schools and the work of educators like Ted Sizer (1984, 1992) and Deborah Meier (1995). Subsequently, Grant Wiggins and Jay McTighe (1998) publicly championed the idea of using essential questions in the design of instructional units, bringing the idea greater visibility in their very popular Understanding by Design curricular framework.
4 Creating an essential question by turning the lesson objective into a question rarely works, and it is a common critique I have of my pre-service teachers' first attempts at submitting lesson plans. "What is mitosis?" and "What are Newton's Laws of motion?"

are not good essential questions because there is no puzzling phenomenon to explain or social issue to be examined in the question itself.

5 This socio-scientific issue approach is exemplified by the scholarship of Dana Zeidler and Troy Sadler (T. D. Sadler & Zeidler, 2004; Zeidler, Sadler, Simmons, & Howes, 2005), and draws upon earlier work in the Science-Technology-Society (STS) movement (e.g. Bybee, 1987; Yager, 1993).

6 Some caution is warranted because the term "problem-based learning" is a label that gets applied to a great deal of teaching, including teaching that is very didactic, and student success may be marked by how closely a solution to a problem comes to a pre-established "right" answer. In a review of the literature on problem-based learning, Merrit et al. (2017) note the absence of consensus on the definition of problem-based learning. In education research, this is what we call a "messy construct" (e.g. Pajares, 1992).

7 Pease & Kuhn, 2011, p. 78.

8 This tradition of work draws upon critical theorists like Paolo Freire (1970, 1985) and examples of the curricular framing discussed here include the work of scholars like Calabrese Barton (2003), Dimick (2012), and Upadhyay (2009), to name just a few.

9 See Morales-Doyle (2017) for a fantastic example of this question serving as the basis for a unit in an Advanced Placement chemistry class.

10 I credit Dr. Cathy Middlecamp from the University of Wisconsin-Madison for introducing me to this incredibly generative essential question when I worked for her as a teaching assistant in her undergraduate chemistry course. I later used it with much success to frame units in my own high school chemistry classes.

11 When a moving car stops, all of its kinetic energy (which is one half its mass times its velocity squared, or $KE = \frac{1}{2} mv^2$) does work on its surroundings. Because the velocity term is squared, doubling the velocity means that the total kinetic energy is quadrupled. All of this gets turned into other forms of work or energy during a crash.

6

RECONSIDERING LABS AND DEMONSTRATIONS FOR MODEL-BASED INQUIRY

Don't Throw Away Those Owl Pellets Just Yet

The student teacher looked up and caught sight of the clock; the change of classes loomed like an approaching storm. "I'm coming around with the trash can," he said. "Please make sure you throw everything away, I don't want to see any owl pellets left on the desk." The students, who had been working attentively, dutifully gathered up the tiny fragments of bone and fur, and used a sponge to wipe down the tabletops. Watching from the back, it was all I could do to stay in my seat. Rarely had I seen such fantastic teaching in an urban science classroom, particularly with so many English language learners, and it broke my heart to see the lab come to such an ignoble end. It felt as if a world-class chef had prepared a meal in front of me, and then tossed most of it into the garbage.

This food, however, had already been eaten by an owl. The undigested bits had been regurgitated into pellets and collected by a science supply company from a forest floor somewhere, then wrapped and sold to high school biology classes around the country. For the past hour, I had watched lab groups open their foil packages and disassemble a lump of material the size and color of a cigar stub. This, students were told, was an owl pellet. The students had slowly dissected their pellets with tweezers and scalpels, finding parts of rodents and various other creatures in them. A key provided by the teacher had helped students keep a running tally on the board of each piece they could identify. Whenever a particularly grisly bit emerged, like a jaw, claw, or feather, all of the students were quickly summoned by the excited group to check it out. Students had been animated by the activity, and even the somewhat squeamish were having a good time. All of this came to a screeching halt at the end of the period.

I have a great deal of sympathy for teachers who run out of time in the middle of interesting science classes, especially when they have been judicious by not squandering the beginning of the period on an unnecessary preamble of instructions, warnings, or tangential lectures. Stopping is not such a big deal with dissections or air track collisions—there is no hardship in putting plastic over a frog or just setting aside gliders until the following day. But to anyone who has ever had students heat test tubes with alcohol burners, trace complex circuits to solve an electrical problem, or count populations of fruit flies, sometimes stopping too soon means needing to start over. There is nothing more frustrating than engaging students in deep and patient work, only to be undermined by the bell.

My critique of this owl pellet lab was different, however, because even though it was laden with scientific possibility, the students stopped just short of actually doing science. Rather than trying to model an ecosystem or learn something about the environment where these owls lived, the students just took the owl pellets apart, made a list of what was there, and called it a day. They had used some of the tools of science to track their data and explore the scientific idea of a food web, but had not done much more than identify the phenomenon under investigation. As I left the room, it felt as if the students had been led right up to the edge of engaging in genuine scientific inquiry, only to retreat at the final moment. How can we as science teachers rethink situations like these, and take up the challenge of redesigning our labs and activities so that students are more engaged in actual scientific practices?[1]

★★★

There is a historical and defining feature of science teaching that seems to cut across all subject areas and grade levels, which may be reduced to the phrase "let me show you something." For generations, there were only a few places most people could see a chunk of sodium explode in water, watch a penny and feather fall together in a vacuum, or witness first-hand observations of micro-organisms. Documentary films and television shows were one source of exposure to these experiences, as were museums, but for most young people, studying science in school was the primary method for gaining access to phenomena that lay beyond the reach of their everyday experiences. Though school science necessarily dealt with helping students examine familiar experiences in new ways, teachers, scientists, and curriculum writers made the inclusion of demonstrations central to their work. They designed lessons and materials specifically with the goal of exposing students to phenomena they had not seen previously. The purpose of a well-designed lecture—like those of Michael Faraday at the Royal Society—was to walk learners through an explanation of what they had just seen.

The spirit of this pedagogy, which I will call *demonstratism* here, lives on in school science in the form of lectures, demonstrations, and laboratory experiences whenever the main purpose of teaching is to expose students to a particular phenomenon or provide a way to think about a particular science idea. And to be fair, the things teachers like to show students can be really interesting. For example, I can vividly recall the first time I saw the thermite reaction rain down molten iron inside a lecture hall. Another demonstration I saw had hundreds of mousetraps in a large glass tank acting as uranium atoms baited with delicately balanced ping-pong balls as neutrons—a single ball was tossed in the tank to start the chain reaction—and this helped me visualize nuclear fission better than anything I had ever read.

A key element of demonstratism, which I will critique here, is that the cognitive load placed on the students is often quite minimal. In some cases, just experiencing the phenomenon is considered an end in itself, with very little being asked of the student other than making observations. This explains how students can spend an afternoon taking apart and looking through owl pellets and only scratch the surface of big disciplinary ideas in ecology.

In the pre-Internet days of limited access to science knowledge, demonstratism may have been a rational philosophy for science teachers, who had access to knowledge and materials that students did not. In these classrooms, demonstrations, laboratory activities, and curated images and videos served the specific purpose of orienting students to the topic by helping students visualize the phenomena.[2] Yet, the idea of a right answer, known by the teacher and unknown to the students, lurks just below the surface of this approach. The practice of beginning the class with a discrepant event—what we might today call a "puzzling phenomenon"—became a commonplace way to engage students' interest by showing them something unexpected. For example, a teacher could rub a balloon on a sweater and then touch it to a fluorescent tube, making it flicker briefly with light.[3]

Science teachers often perform their demonstrations with a degree of showmanship. Done well, these can hook students' interest and motivate them to want to know the answer to the mystery. But they can also take on the appearance of a magic show, placing the scientific understandings at arm's length, even while kindling students' sense of wonder.

In the 21st century, students in our science classes now have less need of all this *showing*. In my own 20th century chemistry classes, I would place a piece of sodium metal the size of a lentil in a shielded beaker of water so my students could see the vigorous reaction on the surface, but now being able to watch online videos of people lobbing softball-sized chunks of sodium into lakes is only a few clicks away.[4] Once upon a time our students needed our slides and videos to see glaciers calving, slow-motion crash testing of cars, and slime molds reproducing. Now they can see these things whenever they want, with or without us. The failure of demonstratism is that even as it may serve to motivate students, just seeing or experiencing phenomena in a science class is no longer enough to foster deep science learning—if it ever even was.

A panel report from the National Academy of Science states that the purpose of school laboratory experiences is to "provide opportunities for students to interact directly with the material world (or with data drawn from the material world), using the tools, data collection techniques, models, and theories of science."[5] In science class, the word "lab" is used as shorthand for a lot of different activities, and the one commonality that connects them is that they all involve active participation from the students. In lab, students are no longer sitting listening to a lecture or taking notes; they are doing something.

There are a lot of different activities that get called "lab." In some of them, the tools, data collection techniques, models, and theories of science are quite evident. In one biology classroom I visited, students rotated from station to station, peering through microscopes and sketching the microorganisms they observed. When my physics students used air track gliders to determine the effect of force on speed, they were engaging in data collection to generate a conceptual model. Some labs require students to follow a set of procedures in order to arrive at a desired end, like the chemistry lab in which copper dust is heated in a crucible and changes color and gains mass, and students must figure out why. Other times, labs aim to teach a specific skill, such as how to perform an acid/base titration using burets and an indicator.

Many teachers talk about activities as if they were the same as labs, but some of these may lack any connection to scientific practices beyond the topic. Part of the issue is the easy conflation of words used to describe school science laboratory activities. Even if an activity takes place at a science workbench, is hands-on, and is pedagogically valuable, it still might not fit the above definition of a laboratory experience.

Plenty of science teachers take advantage of the extra space that a science classroom occasionally affords to spread out, but that does not mean students are necessarily acting like scientists. Sometimes, lab just means taking notes in a different seat. I have seen lots of things called "lab" which probably ought not to have been, such as cutting out photocopied chromosomes and gluing them in pairs, crafting jewelry with rocks polished in a tumbler, and making conservation of energy posters. These were hands-on activities, but engaging in them did not necessarily require students to draw upon the practices of science.

★★★

I had two experiences that started me down the road to rethinking labs. The first was when I was teaching a 9th grade Introductory Physical Science class, and a pair of lab partners had a difficult time getting started.[6] It was a distillation lab in which the students heated a mixture of ethanol and water to find the individual boiling points, and then used that information to separate the liquids using a condensing tube. The two girls had completed their data collection just as the bell rang, and I let them hang back a few minutes to clean up. As we talked, they made it clear that even though they could probably write up the lab report, they now actually understood what they were doing and said they would really like to try doing the lab over. They were persuasive, and the next day they came in and got right to work in the back of the room.

The lab reports they eventually turned in were far above the level of work they had produced for me up to that point. It was clear that doing an entire lab activity more than once had created unforeseen benefits for learning the science.

It was also a lot like real science. When I had worked in an inorganic chemistry lab the previous summer, I often made mistakes that sent me back to square one, but these were productive failures that taught me a great deal about the actual science of what I was doing. They also motivated me, because I finally felt like I knew what I was doing, much like my own students in the distillation lab. The repetition of labs became part of my teaching toolkit from then forward.

The second moment came in teaching a methods course for future science teachers, when one student got mad on behalf of her younger high-school self. "Why does every chemistry lab just end with a white solid?" she asked with visible irritation. She understood concerns about safety and the cost of materials, as well as the obligation for high school chemistry classes to teach students certain laboratory skills and the use of specific tools. It was the lack of imagination in chemistry teaching and the prescriptive nature of lab experiences in school that bothered her. She felt that they were all carefully constrained recipes, even when a procedure allowed for some deviation for inquiry, because there was a right answer at the end—and students were often forced to calculate exactly how far away they were from *that*. I could not disagree.

Some labs are actually quite clever in the way they disguise the science as they deliver the pleasure of a right answer. One old Physical Science Study Committee (PSSC) lab comes to mind, where students measure the curvature of an electron beam in a vacuum tube within a solenoid's magnetic field, then perform some calculations to find the mass of an electron. How could someone not feel like a scientist doing something like that? Of course, it was all a setup, because as long as students made the original measurements within the correct order of magnitude (within a centimeter), the result they were calculating with the provided formulas would produce an answer of the electron's mass that was reasonably close to the answer they could look up. One physics teacher friend—who scrounged vacuum tubes for this activity until the year he retired—gleefully called this a "fake" lab.

★★★

I can recall my chemistry lab in high school, and how our teacher always set out all the materials we needed, but rarely ventured past the edge of the single desks into the sea of black tables to take note of what we were doing. What we were doing in fact was engaging in inquiry with the dropper bottle of 6M nitric acid. My lab partners and I were fascinated by what would react with it (pennies, lab sink fixtures, our skin) and what would not (the cover of the chemistry textbook).

To us at the time, science inquiry meant playing around with random configurations of science materials until something unexpected happened.[7] School science labs—especially in chemistry and physics—were often infused with the notion that one must do them "right," which usually meant that nothing unexpected was going to happen.[8] As a student, I was unable to see any form of systematic scientific investigation between random inquiry and cookbook labs as a way to produce knowledge. It was not until graduate school that I realized the depth of this problem and its relation to a common misunderstanding about the nature of science.

Long before taking high school classes, I had learned the formula for writing lab reports. They began with a title and purpose, followed by a hypothesis, a list of materials, and a sequential procedure. Only once those steps were completed on composition paper in legible handwriting were we permitted to proceed with actually doing something. After a while I decided that it was a way to slow us down so the fun part of the class was not over too quickly. When I became a teacher, this hypothesis was confirmed.

I have since heard this approach referred to as PHEOC—which is short for Problem, Hypothesis, Experiment, Observation, and Conclusion. As a new teacher just trying to survive my first year, I used this same pedagogy uncritically because I knew it would count as teaching science to passing administrators, even if it made me uneasy. The reason PHEOC seemed so attractive—even if I chafed against it as both a student and as a teacher—is that it seemed like it was a guaranteed process for producing knowledge. By dutifully following a series of steps, there was a promise of fully-formed knowledge popping out at the end. In my ignorance, I thought that scientists just messed around doing random experiments until they made knowledge, and when they did, they turned it into a PHEOC-able lab for science classrooms.[9]

While I still think there is value in keeping good records and writing about what happens in the lab, these days I have a difficult time advocating for the PHEOC pedagogy. It seems there are much better ways for teachers to provide opportunities for their students to learn to think scientifically.

★★★

The best laboratory experiences I have witnessed in science classrooms are the ones in which students are involved in sense-making of some kind, rather than just witnessing the science. In these classrooms there is a clear demarcation between the acquisition of a skill needed for a lab—like mounting a slide, calibrating a probe, or using glycerin to insert glass tubing into a stopper—and a genuine experiment that helps students reduce the ambiguity in an explanatory model. Teachers in these classrooms leverage the practices of science at just the right time, teaching metric measurement for example when it is needed, instead of spending weeks on it at the beginning of the year.

These teachers also let students take different pathways—within certain boundaries—in order to ask their own questions and try out their own ideas. Sometimes this means letting go of the belief that every student in a science class needs to be involved in exactly the same learning activities at all times. This one can be tricky, but the results can be glorious.

For example, I do not regret letting Jamilla investigate the relationship between color and wavelength on an old Spec 20 photometer I found in the high school physics storeroom.[10] I excused her from the assignments that the rest of the class was doing, because she was really adamant about wanting to understand the nature of color. It took her a day and a half to realize that she needed to keep track of her readings in a table, but eventually with some coaching she learned to be systematic. Her biggest puzzle was why the readings seemed to be the opposite of what she expected. She had thought that a sample of water with blue food coloring would absorb the blue wavelengths, and red would absorb red, but the opposite happened. I remember her "Aha!" moment on the fourth day when she realized that the apparent color of a solution was the result of wavelengths *not* being absorbed by the sample. In that moment, it was clear that she was learning like a scientist, posing and investigating her questions within a well-defined problem space.

Some science teachers and science education researchers offer a different way of thinking about demonstrations and lab experiences, one more deeply rooted in modern understandings about the way students learn science. This approach—sometimes called *model-based inquiry*—suggests that all science learning ought to begin with a carefully-selected puzzling phenomenon of some kind, and this is where demonstrations can play an important role. The idea is not to just have students figure out the answer, but to develop an explanatory model for the phenomenon. With this approach, the teacher does not play the part of answer-giver, but rather supports students in developing and revising their models, first eliciting students' ideas about the phenomenon and then supporting their construction of a model. Teachers can also introduce scientific ideas along the way that students can include in their models. By making lab about model development and refinement, teachers can offer explicit opportunities for students to connect their existing ideas to the science.[11]

★★★

After the owl pellets were all cleaned up, I readied myself to talk with the cooperating teacher and her student teacher. I thought about what I wished had happened. Throughout the lesson, lots of good questions had come up: what kind of food did the owl's prey eat? How much energy did the owl need to survive, and how much did it have to eat to get it? What did the remains of the prey reveal about the owl's behavior? What patterns existed in the types and quantities of prey? Why wasn't fur digestible?

However, all of these were questions posed by teachers to students, who answered as best as they could. I could not help but feel that if the students had been encouraged to formulate and investigate questions about what they were finding, the owl pellet lab might have taken a little longer and looked much different.[12] And instead of regurgitating fragmented bits and pieces, students would have had a much better chance of digesting the big ideas and practices of science.

Notes

1 The Next Generation Science Standards (Achieve Inc., 2013) adopted in most U.S. states describes eight specific science and engineering practices: asking questions and defining problems, developing and using models, planning and carrying out investigations, analyzing and interpreting data, using mathematics and computational thinking, constructing explanations and designing solutions, engaging in argument from evidence, and obtaining, evaluating, and communicating information.

2 It is amazing to recall the enormous laser-disc machines that were in use in many schools in the 1990s. Though they could also show longer recordings, the discs were quite expensive, and were much more useful as a library of images and video clips. These were marketed to science departments as a technological solution for replacing complicated and potentially dangerous demonstrations.

3 Or drop a dollar bill through the waiting fingers of a student, who would never react fast enough to catch it. Or dip a twenty-dollar bill into a liquid and light it on fire until it turns into a wet twenty-dollar bill. Or mix two chemicals in a flask, and let the students feel how cold the flask gets; then set the flask on a wooden stool with a small secret puddle of water on it that freezes the flask to the stool; then pick up the flask, lifting the stool with it. Or...

4 Whenever I see this, I cannot help but think what a bad idea this is, both for the people and the lakes.

5 The findings from America's Lab Report: Investigations in High School Science (National Research Council, 2006, p. 13) were incorporated into A Framework for K-12 Science Education (National Research Council, 2012).

6 The textbook for the class was Uri Haber-Schaim's Introductory Physical Science (1999), which had been my own textbook as a high school freshman. The approach in the book was very laboratory-based and was derived from the post-war efforts at reforming science education by scientists, specifically the Physical Science Study Committee (Rudolph, 2002). It was not until I had actually used the book for a few years as a teacher that I understood the radical approach to science learning it was really advocating, and I retain a soft spot in my heart for it to this day.

7 This is not so different from the "folk theory of inquiry" that Windschitl (2004) found among his preservice teachers.

8 Except for the lab involving the iodine clock reaction, in which we combined two beakers of clear liquid, waited about fifteen seconds, and then watched the whole thing turn purple all at once. That seemed to be genuine magic. As the lab went on and we were directed to use different concentrations of starch solution, I sadly realized that we were only going to vary the amount of time before the magic happened, instead of trying to figure out how the whole beaker could change from clear to purple instantaneously.

9 Even science stories I thought that I knew well—like the discovery of the iridium layer at the KT boundary and the subsequent theory of dinosaur extinction by meteor (Alvarez, Alvarez, Asaro, & Michel, 1980)—I had assumed were the result of the Alvarez family just poking around. It was not until graduate school that I reconsidered the idea of a what a hypothesis was. Rather than the "educated guess" I had been led to believe, I started thinking of a hypothesis as an if–then statement that could be supported or disconfirmed by evidence from an experiment. For example, Gerta's work on Deccan volcanism as a primary driver of climate change (Gerta et al., 2018) at the KT boundary is driven by the presence of evidence for a much longer extinction event that preceded the Chicxulub meteor impact. If the large mass extinction peaked prior to the impact, then the meteor was not the causal event of the mass extinction.

10 Even though I am using pseudonyms throughout this book, I will gently let it slip that she figured out that her last name was a color whose wavelength she could measure.

She told me that 520 Nanometers was her new "tag" around school, and even signed her physics papers "Jamilla 520nm" for the rest of the year.

11 In a comprehensive review of the state of inquiry in science education, Duschl and Grandy (2008) note the contemporary shift from "a view of science that emphasizes observation and experimentation, to a view that stresses theory and model building and revision," (p. 9).

12 I wondered if the owl pellets were from wild or captive owls. And if they were captive, did the supply company have the owls on specific diets to produce interesting pellets for school science labs?

7

WHAT IF THE STORK CARRIED 20-SIDED DICE?

On the Use of Models and Simulations as Tools for Thinking

Anjali's students circled around her in the school's multi-purpose room while she explained the rules of the population ecology simulation, but because they were 7th graders, they fidgeted while she talked. Eventually some even sat down as the direction-giving lasted longer than their patience. Anjali's cooperating teacher stood to the side for support, nodding along and giving non-verbal behavior reminders to certain students, eventually marching one into the hallway for a private reprimand about being on his phone.

Like many classroom simulations, this one assigned each student a role, and Anjali had put masking tape on the floor to mark the edges of the "pond," and gave each student a badge to help keep everyone clear about whether they were starting out as a predator (big fish), prey (little fish), or a resource (food for the little fish). There were a lot of rules, but the main thing students needed to know was that when they died in the game, they became something else. Food became little fish, little fish became big fish, and big fish who starved came back into the environment as food. The time units of the game were measured in steps, and one of the students helpfully suggested that each large square tile on the floor could serve as a single step. Anjali, standing next to a large whiteboard ready to record population data after every 5 steps, agreed this was a good idea, and had the students take their places to begin the simulation.

In short order, a model of pond population dynamics unfolded in real time. Some of the predators made immediately for little fish, while a few little fish found edges of the pond where they would be safe and near the food. One little fish took out his phone again. Soon there were too many big fish, and they began to starve. After about ten minutes of real time, each of the populations had peaked and crashed a few times. Anjali kept things going for a little while longer, and then let the students sit down in front of the whiteboard to copy the data into their notebooks. The previous night, Anjali and I had talked about possible directions to take this end-of-class discussion, and she had decided to circle the students again to talk about the patterns they were seeing in the data, and how this related to real ponds.

The discussion was wonderful, and I left that observation feeling good about Anjali as a new teacher. However, I also had a nagging thought that an opportunity had been missed. In the ten years since that observation I have had plenty of time to think about that missed opportunity, and I have decided that it has to do with the nature of simulations as a type of model, and the willingness of teachers to let their students change the rules of the game. The minor timekeeping suggestion by the student was the clue.

★★★

It is no exaggeration to say that model development and revision are defining features of scientific inquiry. Models can have lots of different forms—graphs, equations, written or verbal descriptions, simulations, schematic diagrams, chemical formulas, etc.—and what each has in common is the ability to represent how different parts of observable phenomena relate to one another. It is not incorrect to say that *model* is now largely synonymous with the scientific meaning of *theory*. [1]

Our modern understanding of science requires that models undergo revisions as the need arises in order to better incorporate new data or refine predictions; they are not frozen in time like the ideas of Aristotle and Ptolemy in the middle ages. When there are gaps or uncertainties in a model, a well-designed experiment can offer hints on how to refine or revise the model so that it has more explanatory power. A model can also be overhauled entirely when it is unable to accommodate or explain anomalous data. [2]

Simulation games are fun, and when done well, engage the students by making them players inside the model. I have seen many varieties of the population ecology simulation I observed that day in Anjali's class, and all of them attempt to illuminate the complex relationships between organisms and their environment. One simulation of natural selection uses different types of tweezers or spoons for "finches" to pick up "food," typically represented by beads. Chemistry classes all over the world simulate the idea of half-life and nuclear decay by putting coins in a box, shaking it vigorously, and removing all the ones flipped to one particular side. Nearly every physics teacher I know makes bountiful use out of the wonderful collections of science simulations that can be run on web browsers. All of these simulations produce data that can be examined for patterns by students, and many of the novice teachers with whom I work see the simulation as an end in itself; they are not wrong when they view the activity and engagement of the students as worthwhile.

Using models to generate the kinds of data similar to those measured from actual phenomena in the real world allows students to gain insight into the ways in which those actual phenomena operate over time. Yet all too often, science teachers stop short of using these models to their fullest potential, because they only focus on what the model explains, instead of also looking at what the model does not explain. Simple models—sometimes called "first-approximation models"—are important because they allow students to understand how the representation (big fish, little fish, food) maps onto the real world (carp, trout, bass, perch, minnows, plants, algae, etc.). This allows students to use the model as a tool for thinking about the relationships between the different parts. However, students can go much deeper if pressed to think about revising the model itself.

In simulations, this means rethinking the *rules* in consideration of real-world data. If students are asked to figure out how they might change the rules, and the parts of the model, to make the simulation more "realistic," what they are really doing is revising the model based upon what they know about the real-life phenomena under consideration.

There are two ways to approach changing simulations. The first is to keep the existing pieces of the model and just alter the parameters enough to adjust the fit. For example, making the pond simulation more realistic might mean looking at things like how fast the predators move (maybe 2 steps per turn instead of 1?), or how much food is needed to survive. A modification of this type might look at data that shows predator populations decreasing shortly after a prey population crash. If the simulation gives a different output, students can propose changes that might make the simulation run with greater fidelity to the data. In computer simulations, this is usually a matter of changing the value of a few variables, or moving around a slider.

A second approach to changing the rules would be to include other real-world factors that are not yet a part of the model. In Anjali's pond, these might be seasonal changes, more food sources, or additional organisms. This is where games are more flexible than computer simulations—at least in schools—because giving new instructions to a group of students is much faster and easier than incorporating those rules into operational computer code. If the simulation is a game, like in Anjali's class, a revision to the rules is an opportunity to run the new simulation and play the game again to see how the outcome differs. Given adequate time, an ambitious teacher can adjust the parameters of the existing simulation *and* change the rules.

★★★

Sometimes in school science, teachers operate from a basic conception of modeling that only seeks to represent the phenomenon. Kids love making organelles out of frosting and fondant, but if the end purpose of a cake model of a cell is just to look at it (or eat it), then the learning outcomes are limited to definition and memorization. Scientists use models as tools for reasoning, and this is a worthy goal for their use in science classrooms too. A good question to ask ourselves whenever we are asking students to construct a model is whether or not we intend our students to *do* something with it. If the answer is no, then maybe it is just for decoration.

One simulation I observed in an environmental science class used dice to represent human population growth: a roll of 5 or 6 indicated a birth, 1 a death, and 2, 3, or 4 meant no population change. The teacher had designated one student as the "stork," and as new babies were "born" with each turn, the student walked around with a big bucket from which he adjusted the balance of dice to each group based on their net gain or loss of population.[3]

As I watched the simulation unfold, I thought about the givens of the situation. With a two in six chance of a birth, and a one in six chance of a death each time the students rolled their dice, the growth rate in this simulation was about 17%, reflecting the underlying probability statistics of an average of one birth each turn for every six people. Pedagogically, this seemed like a reasonable simplification in order to teach the idea of population growth. And indeed, when the students aggregated their class data, they were able to construct a curve that showed the exponential growth of their population of dice, and this idea became part of the larger environmental science discussions subsequently in the class.

And yet, what if the lesson had not stopped there? What if instead of just portraying endless exponential growth, the students had been tasked with modeling actual populations? A quick glance at worldwide population statistics show that the largest growth rates for countries are around 3%, with a few small outliers at 4 or 5%. A number of other countries—including the United States—actually have negative growth rates in the same range. What if students had been tasked with coming up with a way to model these actual rates? What if they were encouraged to more clearly define what they meant by a turn—was it a year? a decade? a generation? What if that bucket had a bunch of different polyhedral dice (with 8, 12, 20, or even 60 sides)? What if they looked at different sized countries for multiple years? Or developed different models that incorporated various factors like the wealth of a country, whether it was at peace, etc.?

Instead of uncritically accepting a simplistic population model as an illustration of one facet of the course content, the students could be offered a first-approximation model that they were expected to revise and expand in order to give it more explanatory power. In this way, the students would genuinely be engaging in the same type of work done by scientists because the models they built and revised would be part of the toolkit they deployed to better understand the world.[4]

★★★

Hidden just below the surface of this seemingly technical discussion about the pedagogy of modeling in science classes is a very powerful idea that has infused modern thinking for the past few centuries: namely, that we do not have to uncritically accept the validity of knowledge on the basis of authority alone.

When presented with evidence from phenomena themselves, human beings may in fact choose to build or modify their existing explanations and interpretations. This was true of Christians during the Lutheran Reformation who revised their interpretations of religious texts, astronomers during the Copernican revolution who revised interpretations of scientific data, and of scholars during the Enlightenment who reexamined long-held assumptions about human social organization and governance. As a species we have fought for the right to be able to use our minds to hack into existing explanatory models and reconfigure them in ways that work better for us. From this perspective, providing students with an opportunity to approach knowledge critically, with express permission to adjust the rules in an attempt to better fit the data, resonates nicely with the requirements of civic engagement in a democratic society.

Notes

1 As a consequence of persistent attacks by those opposed to the teaching of evolution in public schools in the United States, the word theory has become colloquially redefined as a pejorative that refers to a conjecture sown with doubt about its own plausibility (Branch & Mead, 2008).

2 I am particularly fond of historical case studies of scientific inquiry that explore what this idea looks like in practice. Examples include Conant's (1951) story about the development of the concept of atmospheric pressure, Kuhn's (1970) use of phlogiston and impetus as exemplars of overturned paradigms, Haraway's (1989) discussion of how female primatologists forced a reinterpretation of long-held assumptions, Scerri's (2013) modern re-examination of the development of the periodic table, and the cases assembled by Collins and Pinch (1998), Gieryn (1999), and Latour and Woolgar (1979) that draw attention to the role of credibility in assessing or overturning knowledge claims. All of these show science as a profoundly human activity—after all, we are the ones demanding explanations for anomalous data.

3 In U.S. popular culture the "stork" has historically represented a first-approximation model of human reproduction offered by parents who do not wish to discuss human sexuality and childbirth with their children. It has no empirical backing, is barely intelligible as a model, and the only phenomena it explains is the sudden appearance of new babies in a family. Yet it still superior in explanatory power to the other major animal-based model in U.S. culture—that of the predictive power of groundhogs over the length of the northern hemisphere's winter season as represented in the Groundhog Day celebration every February 2nd.

4 It is also the case that sometimes the methods and materials we use for models reflect back on the phenomena in unexpected ways. The school in this example was located in a primarily white community where I had earlier detected a hostile climate toward students of color, many of whom were bussed in from a neighboring district. I sat with a group of white students whose dice were all blue for the first few minutes, until they had two births. The stork came around and put two yellow dice on the table. One person in the group said, "Racism!" Then, pointing to a yellow die, he said, "That one must be Chinese!" "Yeah, you just adopted two kids," said the stork. This exchange was overheard by the other students at the table, but not the teacher. Sometimes I think racism is like corrosive radioactive waste that just leaks out of whatever container it is stored in. The manner in which it just burst into this little essay about modeling is reflective of the same way it explodes without warning into our students' lives. It even happens the very science classrooms where nice white science teachers tell me all the

time that race has nothing to do with science teaching. The intellectual challenge for science teachers in a situation like this is deciding what to say or do in the moment when something like this happens in their presence. I do not have a pre-packaged answer, but I do know that not responding at all only serves to perpetuate racism. With my own students, I find that role-playing various approaches to such situations allows them to generate, test, and compare different possible responses, and perhaps be more prepared to intervene in the moment when racism leaks into their classrooms, as it inevitably will.

8

EYES LIKE A SCIENTIST

Framing Safety as Part of Scientific Practice for Students

There is an element of danger about science that is attractive to some students and induces anxiety in others. For certain, science is associated with Ebola virus, nuclear weapons, earthquakes, deadly neurotoxins, and other threats to life and limb. If it is unsafe, somewhere scientists are studying it. That danger easily extends into the science classroom, and science teachers are well aware that an oversight on their part could actually result in student injury. As teachers, we are the adults in charge—*in loco parentis*, as the lawyers say—and are responsible for our students' safety even as we introduce the risk. English teachers worry less about this sort of thing.

When I was a student, I hated goggles, even though I knew I had to wear them to protect my eyes in lab. They fogged up, left marks on my face, and generally got in the way of me clearly seeing what I was doing. I was less hostile toward lab aprons; they at least helped me keep my clothes clean. It was not until I was a student teacher that I started thinking about goggles as anything other than a necessary annoyance. During a lab, when one of my students put on her goggles and apron for the first time, she smiled and said, "I feel like a scientist." I interpreted this as the sort of remark anyone playing dress-up might make, pleasant, yet trivial. My cooperating teacher arched her brow and looked at me like I was supposed to say something. When I did not, she turned to the student and responded, "That's because you *are* a scientist."[1] I am sure I had previously heard something about nurturing students' identities as scientists in one of my courses, but I did not fully understand the idea until that moment.

The benefit of having students wear safety goggles is that they protect their eyes as well as their teachers' livelihoods. Further, this practice also instills in students one of the most important values of engaging in science and engineering, that of mitigating risk and maintaining a safe environment in which to work. As a student, I once viewed safety goggles as a barrier between the science and me. Now, I see them as an element of the toolkit for inquiry.

★★★

As a relatively new teacher, an appeal to authority felt like the path of least resistance. I taped a photocopied regulation to the goggle cabinet, given to me by another chemistry teacher who had found it a useful defense for her insistence that the kids wear safety goggles in the lab. Still, I was not very good at enforcing my goggle policy, and every so often in lab a student would end up at the eyewash station, while a few students would joke about me getting sued for it.[2] Finally I just laid down the law: everyone always wears goggles in the lab. No exceptions. This would lead to exchanges like the following:

STUDENT: I hate these things. They give me raccoon eyes. Why do we have to wear them?

TEACHER: Because you're boiling water. And it's New Jersey state law.

STUDENT: Oh, like I really wear goggles at home when I boil water for mac and cheese, Mr. Larkin.

Over time, I learned to see the role of goggles in labs differently. Goggles serve an important signaling function to students that safety is an integral part of the practice of *real* science, not just *school* science. Like wearing seatbelts in a car, the issue goes beyond compliance with a law. It reduces the chances of injury in the event there is an accident, and we know there will be accidents. I will never forget the time a student had a seizure in the lab area of the classroom while my students were boiling sodium hydroxide in beakers over open flames—thankfully no one was hurt, but it could have been a much worse situation.

My advice these days for science teachers is to signal to students that safety practices are an integral part of scientific inquiry and engineering. In my work as a science teacher educator, I have had the opportunity to visit a number of research and manufacturing facilities, and in each place the importance of safety has been visible on every surface.[3] Though ever-present, these messages were not coercive or rooted in obedience to authority. The implicit message in these institutional practices is that when the working environment is not safe, things go wrong, people get hurt, and the project suffers.

Of course, there are more direct consequences for unsafe working conditions and practices like higher insurance premiums, workers' compensation, lawsuits, and fines from state and federal regulators. Certainly, these are necessary backstops to ensure that regulations and safe practices are followed, but the bigger idea is that a safe working environment is good for science.

Framed this way, safety is more than just an ethical or legal obligation; it is a way to ensure that science goes on.

As science teachers, we can also deal out our consequences for non-compliance, but it is always worth fostering students' internal motivation by framing the wearing of goggles (and adherence to other safety guidelines) in terms of an ethic of mutual responsibility, and as an integral part of the practice of science. This seems preferable to framing a goggle policy as simple adherence to state law, as I did as a new teacher.

★★★

Part of what makes the enforcement of goggle rules difficult is that circumstances can easily turn oppositional when students resist, and a coercive approach to safety may actually backfire. If we treat lab as a reward for engaging students in the less exciting parts of class, and then turn lab into a chore anyway, then adding on one more oppressive rule about goggles may cause students to feel that doing science is simply not worth the hassle.

As a teacher, I have found the most success by having a "one warning" policy, after which the students take a short time out, and if it happens again, a long time out.[4] Some teachers have very strict policies, while other teachers—usually new ones—are a bit more lax in their goggle policy because they want to choose their battles carefully.[5] They might wonder if it is it really worth having a confrontation over goggles with a challenging student who is deeply engaged in the lab activity. This is where minimalist strategies can come in very handy. Looking directly at the student and tapping my own goggles is usually enough, though sometimes just saying the word "goggles" will do.[6] Occasionally, I will playfully inform my students that I have a very peculiar auditory disorder which causes me not to hear them if they are not wearing goggles. I generally tend to avoid sarcasm in the classroom because it tends to wear away at the trust necessary for open communication with students, but this strategy has worked unexpectedly well.

Goggles can work as a signifier of real science at all levels, not just in high school science laboratories. I have had numerous occasions to counsel teachers, administrators, and science departments in elementary and middle schools who are working toward more student-centered and inquiry-based approaches to science teaching. Often in these places, there has already been a degree of upheaval and change, and it is not unusual to find lab rooms or warehouses with unboxed science kits or supplies. In situations like these, the most pressing question is where to start. My advice is usually the same: find a set of safety goggles for the classroom, set aside some spares for later, and install a goggle cabinet. Then give students the opportunity to act and feel like scientists.

Yet, there is a compelling critique that this whole business of "goggles as a signifier of science" is problematic. Part of the reason students feel like scientists when they put on goggles is that dominant cultural images of science and scientists are skewed toward a particular vision of what counts as science and who is able to do it.[7] There is a great deal of authentic scientific inquiry that gets done without goggles, and we do our students a disservice if we as science teachers depict scientists and the practice of science as only existing within such a narrow frame.[8]

★★★

I want to end this chapter with a brief story about safety goggles and an unexpected opportunity to leverage one student's home life and culture into a science teaching moment. During my first year of teaching, I received a copy of a demonstration intended to scare students into wearing their goggles. It seemed so weird that I never thought about actually doing it, but I often read the procedure to my students. The demonstration required only a cow eyeball—anatomically similar to the human eye—and a little sulfuric acid, and was designed to simulate what would happen in the event of a laboratory accident.

One year I did not get around to telling my students about this demonstration until December, when my third period class was being particularly careless about wearing goggles. I had been forced to pull a few kids out of the lab after multiple warnings, which I hated doing. The next day I gave a long-winded goggle speech and mentioned the cow-eye demonstration. It was no longer the beginning of the year, and the students were less timid then they had been in September. They began to badger me that we should actually do that demonstration in class. "Sorry folks," I said. "But where am I going to get cow eyes?"

Sara, a girl in the second row raised her hand. She was normally very quiet, so I rightly suspected I was going to be obligated to walk my talk. "My dad runs a slaughterhouse," she said sweetly, "I'm sure if I ask him he'll give you some cow eyes." Indeed, her father ran a small Halal butchery, and as a result of this suggestion, she would also get the chance to explain a bit about Islam and Halal food practices to her classmates. Following my visit to get the cow eyes, we came to know her family well, and did our Indo-Pak shopping at their store a few blocks from our house in Trenton, New Jersey.

A few days later, I arrived early for school with a small Styrofoam cooler in hand. I stood at my desk about an hour before the students arrived, trying to figure out exactly how I was going to do the demo. With goggles on, I slipped on a latex glove and gingerly plunged my hand in to the bag of cow eyes. They were the size of ping-pong balls and felt like peeled hard-boiled eggs. I tried really hard not to be grossed out as I let a drop of concentrated sulfuric acid fall onto the cornea of one I had managed to grasp, and within a few seconds it turned from clear to cloudy-white. Nothing more dramatic than that happened, but I knew that for the safety message to get across to students, nothing else needed to happen, either.

Only Sara's class knew the demonstration was coming, all of the others had to guess what was in the cooler first.[9] First I had them put on their goggles, and then I walked around the desks and showed them each an unblemished bovine eye. Then I dabbed the acid on it and carried it around again, with a fresh eye for comparison. They were sickeningly awestruck, and I knew I would never have a goggle problem again. Indeed, I did not. "This is the coolest thing I've seen," said my number-one behavior problem. "If you did stuff like this every day I would be your *best* student."

Notes

1 My cooperating teacher was Mistilina Sato, who at the time was a middle school teacher in suburban New Jersey and is now a renowned education researcher and assessment expert at the University of Canterbury in New Zealand. I was very lucky.

2 Throughout my career, I have encountered teachers who refuse to do any labs at all that involve a need for safety goggles or the use of open flames, citing a desire to avoid student injury and lawsuits. In schools with substandard lab facilities and missing safety equipment, this may be a rational choice. Still, it always seems that there are other science teachers in the school who figure out ways to do their labs activities safely or better yet, pressure their school into addressing the safety concerns.

3 For the past few summers, my colleague Dr. Sandra Adams and I have brought our preservice science teachers in the Montclair Noyce Teacher Scholarship Program to sites throughout New Jersey, including Picatinny Arsenal, the Meadowlands Environmental Research Institute, Pfizer's stability testing laboratories, a power generation plant run by PSE&G, Panasonic's Newark headquarters as well as other places. I also recently visited the National Magnetic Laboratory while visiting Florida State University in Tallahassee, and my wife Melissa and I toured the small but fascinating Hillestad Pharmaceuticals plant while on vacation in Woodruff, Wisconsin. Obviously, I still like field trips.

4 The psychology is similar to that used in designing passcode protection on a phone that locks the user for five minutes after three failed attempts, and then fifteen minutes after a fourth, etc.

5 One new chemistry teacher I worked with had a very difficult time getting his students to wear their goggles, and I pointed out to him that he often wore his on his head during lab. Adolescents have a strong sense of identifying hypocritical behavior among adults, and may justify their own actions by pointing to an adult doing the same thing.

6 The importance of using of non-verbal cues or single word phrases for classroom management cannot be overstated. I have found the suggestions from Faber and Mazlish (2008) to be incredibly helpful on this point. Sometimes—as any student can confirm—we adults just talk too much.

7 In the first studies using the Draw-a-Scientist Test conducted with about 5,000 children in the 1960s and 70s (Chambers, 1983), only 28 students (less than 1%) drew a female scientist. A recent meta-analysis of 5 decades of "Draw-a-Scientist" studies that focused on gender (D. I. Miller, Nolla, Eagly, & Uttal, 2018) recently found that depictions of scientists in the test have become more gender diverse but that the majority of scientists drawn by students remain male, and this percentage increases as students age. In the over 20,000 student drawings of scientists reviewed for this study: "50% of drawn scientists had laboratory coats, 38% had eyeglasses or goggles, 78% were indoors or in a laboratory, 18% were middle-aged or older, and 79% were Caucasian on average," (p. 1951).

8 Take for example Snively and Corsiglia's (2001) description of the traditional ecological knowledge of the Nisga'a people of British Columbia: "Among the Nisga'a, and among other aboriginal peoples, formal observation, recollection, and

consideration of extraordinary natural events is taken seriously...Nisga'a observers traditionally use all of their senses and pay attention to important variables: what plants are in bloom, what birds are active, when specific animals are migrating and where, and so forth. In this way, traditional communities have a highly developed capacity for building up a collective data base. Any deviations from past patterns are important and noted." (p. 19).

9   "Mr. Larkin! I thought you were a vegetarian!" said one ninth-grader that day. I have always found it touching when students show awareness of their teachers as actual people. "I'm not going to eat it," I told her.

9

IN PRAISE OF FIELD TRIPS AND GUEST SPEAKERS

Bringing the Inside-Out and the Outside-In for Science Learning

The research scientist from Princeton Plasma Physics Laboratory had just finished explaining the difference between the kind of plasma in the sun, and the type of plasma produced in the reactor at the lab where he worked, and asked if the students had any questions. The hands of my juniors and seniors shot up across the room, and he called on a student in the front row.

"I still don't understand this whole thing about Pluto not being a planet. How can they say that Pluto isn't a planet?"

After a momentary pause, the speaker did his best to answer, but he was clearly flummoxed by the fact that the question had nothing to do with what he had just talked about for twenty minutes. The small plasma ball he had plugged into the outlet on my desk at the front still crackled blue sparks. He called on another student.

"They say that the universe goes on forever, but then they also say that it's getting bigger. How is that possible? Like, it's already infinite so how can something get bigger than that?" The physicist looked over at me and I just shrugged. Before the class was over, he also had to explain why the sky was blue.

As much as we try to convince them otherwise, it is quite common for students not to see their teachers as scientists. Given the opportunity to meet "real" scientists, many students think it is fair game to ask them any science question. After all, people who call themselves scientists must know lots of things about science, right?

I had seen this phenomenon before, and it delighted me every time. It had even happened to me when I went into my son's kindergarten class to do a demonstration on how leaves change color in the fall.[1] Once the questions started, the kindergarteners only wanted to talk about bears.

.★★★

Inviting guest speakers into class is always a little bit of a hassle, especially if you want someone to speak with more than one class, but I have always found them to be worthwhile disruptions of the daily routine. More than that, they are welcome intrusions of the real world into the artificial environment of school.

As a third grader, I can recall studying Hawai'i—I was infatuated with volcanoes. My grandparents had visited the islands and had taken home movies of the volcanoes erupting. My grandpa came into class and showed those movies and talked a little about what things they had seen in Hawai'i. He had footage of my grandmother walking along a black sand beach—quite a contrast to the experiences of my classmates and I to the white sands of the Jersey shore. I was so proud of my grandpa that day, and school felt like the best place in the world. Though it was always a little more difficult as a high school teacher, I was always open to having my students suggest family and friends who could come in to talk to a class.

My other early history with guest speakers comes from experiences as a high school student in a senior government class. We often had guest speakers, many of whom were candidates for local office. In this class it was our responsibility as students to contact and "host" the speakers, and I remember that my big achievement was inviting a county official who eventually became mayor of Trenton. It was this experience as a student that led me to want to continue this practice as a teacher, even if I was teaching physics instead of civics.

In my first year teaching, I noticed that we did not have Veterans Day off. This caught my attention because of a conversation I had earlier that fall with a veteran outside my apartment building. He told me that he was on his way to the VA hospital for treatment, and that he suffered from Agent Orange poisoning.[2] This conversation had a powerful effect on me, and afterward I thought about the ways in which it might link to chemistry class. I thought it might be a good idea to see if there were any veterans who were interested in coming to my class, so in late October I called the state Department of Veterans Affairs, and I was surprised to be connected to the director, Dave Martin, almost immediately.[3] When I asked if he could suggest anyone who might be interested in talking to students about Agent Orange, he said that he would do it.

On Veterans Day, I met Dave in the main office along with another veteran he had brought along, and I walked them to my class. They began by hanging large survey maps of Vietnam on the front board, with yellow highlighter over the areas where Agent Orange had been sprayed. They talked about being in Vietnam, and what the day-to-day life of a soldier there was like, and then spent a good fifteen minutes talking about the way Agent Orange was used as a defoliant so that the Viet Cong would have less jungle in which to hide. My students started asking a range of questions: why was the government spraying poison? How did it know whether its own soldiers were being sprayed or not? Why did soldiers have to keep returning to the same areas over and over again? They answered as best as they could, and I chimed in whenever we got deep into the chemistry (which honestly, was not that often). It was every bit the powerful experience for students that I had hoped it would be, something I could tell by how serious my usual class jokers had been. The next day one of my students told me that her dad had been in Vietnam, but had never talked about it, but when she came home and told him about the guest speakers, they had their first real conversation about his experiences.

Of course, not every speaker is going to connect with students this way. I once invited a performance artist to visit my ninth-grade physical science class. His art was made by high voltage lines that ran through special gloves with pointed metal tips, and blue sparks emanated from his fingers, traveling through paper to a grounded easel. It was amazing to watch, and I thought my students would love it. They did, but there was not as much of a scientific connection I had hoped, and after about fifteen minutes it turned into an art lesson that only engaged a handful of students.

Over the years, I have had many guest speakers, and my self-imposed standard has been to try to have one for each class I teach every year. Inviting in guest speakers is something I continue to do even now in my university classes—and sometimes the best guest speakers for future teachers are the students themselves. One year, I taught a student teaching seminar in a middle school and asked the school's guidance counselor for help in assembling a student panel for the class. I had asked him if we could just get the group of students that challenge him the most, and he knew just who to ask. When the seventh graders walked into the room, my student teachers were prepared with questions, but were quickly set straight. "Put away your questions," one girl said, "I know you got stuff you want to ask, but we got stuff we want to TELL you." Later on, once they really got going, she said, "And another thing...Why do you teachers always give us a second chance to do stuff? If we didn't want to do it the first time, what makes you think we're going to want to do it the second time?" It was one of the most amazing 40-minutes of my life.

One student teacher I once supervised decided to be his own guest speaker. Brendan started his 9th grade biology class with a few updates about the upcoming genetics and DNA units, before announcing that there would be a guest speaker. "I'll be right back," he told them, "He's waiting in the biology office." Brendan left the room briefly, and returned wearing the brown robes of a monk. "Let me introduce myself. My name is Johann Gregor Mendel..." he began. For the next forty minutes, "Mr. Mendel" recounted his own life story, along with a detailed account of his experiments with pea plants.[4]

Modern technology makes it even easier to bring the outside in. For example, my colleague at Montclair State University, Jackie Willis, runs a program called *Rainforest Connections* that uses interactive videoconferencing to connect scientists working in Panama (and elsewhere) with classrooms around the world. Museums and science centers in particular are now doing some amazing work in reaching out to scientists and connecting them with students of all ages.[5]

Some of the pragmatic issues still remain with virtual guest speakers: for example, if you teach five sections of chemistry it is often not practical to try to get someone to repeat the same talk five times in a row. And though a single conversation can easily be recorded and replayed for later classes, everyone knows the experience is not the same. Likewise, if the room is too large, or technical glitches plague the conversation, students might come away from the experience discouraged. This is a worthwhile risk however, because there is something delightful about the authenticity of a conversation directly between students and a scientist however it occurs.

★★★

If guest speakers represent bringing the outside world into the classroom, then field trips are the exact opposite. They are intrusions of the school world into real life. Field trips are hard to pull off; most require extensive planning, permission slips, arranging transportation, handling money, and securing approval from administrators who are all too aware of how badly things can go wrong once students are outside the confinement of the school building.[6]

The argument in favor of field trips is a simple one: students learn things on field trips that they might not otherwise learn, especially when they visit places they would not necessarily go on their own. It also helps when some thought has been put into the learning experiences students are intended to have. Families and school administrators alike will agree that if a teacher is taking students on field trip, it had better be worth it.

In the continuum of all possible field trips, students do not really consider going outside to collect data or doing a demonstration to be in the category of the field trip, but it remains the easiest to do.[7] I have taken physics students outside to measure a tower's height by its shadow's length, biology students to the edge of the school sports field to do a square meter environmental survey, and walked my Kenyan students over to the school's borehole pump to make sense of water pressure. Each brief excursion outside has been a welcome respite from the predictable patterns of daily school life for students and teacher alike.

Then there are the trips that are within walking distance, but beyond school grounds. I once accompanied a student teacher in an environmental science class on a walk to a nearby park for an orienteering activity, and another time brought my own chemistry students over to the hospital across the street from the high school. For these, it is worth remembering that an easy walking distance for one person may not be so simple for another, and that transportation may still need to be arranged for some students.

Often the best trips are to places that are accustomed to receiving students, and have an educational experience already prepared. Museums, zoos, aquariums, and science centers are generally structured around informal learning activities, and simply require that the students are adequately chaperoned and well-behaved in order for them to have the best experiences. Like many teachers, I have a loose definition of chaperone—parents, aunts and uncles, grandparents, older siblings, other teachers who could use a day out of the classroom—as long as there is room on the bus or they can meet us there, teachers are always happy to have other adults around help keep things running smoothly.[8] Many places offer free or reduced cost chaperone tickets for the same reason.

One constraint for field trips besides money is time. Often, for reasons beyond anyone's control, trips have to take place within the span of the regular school day. If buses or public transportation run late, or there is traffic, or the location is distant, trips can get unexpectedly cut short. Sometimes a brief visit is fine. When I was a student teacher I went with my eighth graders on a trip that was an hour on the bus, an hour pulling fossils from a creek bed, and an hour home. It was the perfect amount of time for the trip. In contrast, the day I was stuck with my ninth graders all morning on the New Jersey Turnpike, and had only an hour at Liberty Science Center before we had to head back was not really worth the expenditure of time and effort. Such is the risk of venturing out beyond the classroom.[9]

Some field trip settings offer curricular materials that can help make more authentic connections to the science that the students are studying in school. I particularly appreciated the materials from Six Flags that I was able to integrate into lessons throughout the year in preparation for the Physics Day trip we had planned for the spring.[10] By the time students were at the top of the Free Fall ride, they knew that if they timed the drop, they could estimate the height of the ride with the formula $d=5t^2$.

There are also really big trips that span multiple days. During the 1970s and 80s, many school districts sent their middle school students on environmental retreats for 3–4 days at a time.[11] While a few districts still bring students on overnight trips, many do not, and even ones that continue this tradition have shifted away from a science education mission and instead have organized them around teambuilding and outdoor leisure activities. In some places, upper-level science elective courses offer the possibility of trips, but these can be expensive and an optional part of a course. These kinds of trips are possible for science teachers, but they can take years of planning and preparation. They also take a strong commitment to equity in order to ensure that they are not just for the students who can afford them.

★★★

Though they can be a hassle and take time away from other kinds of instruction, bringing guest speakers into the classroom and taking students on field trips can provide new and unforeseen pathways for students to access the ideas we want them to learn, and ultimately they are worth the trouble they take to plan and accomplish. Including these experiences for students in our work as science teachers serves to enrich the curriculum beyond the boundaries of what we can directly control. By putting school science to the test of surviving contact with the real world, guest speakers and field trips are sources of both randomness and authenticity that ultimately strengthen students' relationship with scientific concepts. When guided by thoughtful science teachers, bringing the inside–out and the outside–in serves to enrich the field of ideas that students draw upon as they make sense of science in their classrooms.

Notes

1 Here is the idea I presented to the students, adapted from a workshop I had attended at a science teachers' convention: to prepare, I drew an outline in the shape of a leaf on the whiteboard, and the teacher and I taped 30 green balloons inside the leaf, along with 10 yellow, 5 orange, and 5 red ones, all intermixed. When the kids sat on the carpet in front of the board, I told a story about how these balloons were like the colored pouches that made energy inside the leaf, and how as the weather got cooler, some of the colors stopped getting food from the tree and faded away. Then, I had students come to the board one-by-one and pop the green balloons with a pin. Once the green ones were all gone, I asked them to describe how this leaf might look. Then we popped the yellow balloons, etc. The idea that I hoped the students would take away was that the colors were already there in the leaf, and that by changing color, leaves were simply showing what was there all along. This is, of course, a very rough first-approximation model. The story gets quite a bit more complicated for the red colors.

2 I had only a vague understanding of what that was, and as I asked questions, he eventually lifted up the back of his shirt and showed me the tell-tale chloracne nodules that continued to erupt from his back decades after his exposure to Agent Orange in Vietnam. He had seen the American plane fly directly overhead and spray his whole unit.

3 I had no idea at the time that Dave was the twin brother of my high school government teacher, Doug Martin. They both served as Marines in Vietnam, Dave first, then Doug, in the late 1960s. Dave's book, Crazy Asian War (2008), under his not-so-secret pseudonym "Smilie," is a raw and powerful chronological account of his Vietnam experience.

4 The content of the lecture was organized, and he did a good job with presenting the history and nature of scientific inquiry. I personally found the lecture interesting, but quickly realized that it was not adapted for a ninth-grade audience. At the beginning of "Mr. Mendel's" presentation, many students seemed to be actively listening, but over the course of the period it became difficult for some of them to remain focused on the lecture, and they clearly were unsure of what they were supposed to be doing while Mr. Mendel talked. I gave Brendan full marks for creativity, but even he recognized that the students probably had not learned what he intended.

5 For decades, certain science research grants awarded by the U.S. governmental agencies have been required to demonstrate that they include efforts to ensure a broader impact of the project beyond the research team itself. Many of these grant recipients, such as Palmer Station Antarctica and the JASON project, as well as agencies like NASA and the Department of Energy, offer opportunities for students and teachers to interact directly with scientists in various ways.

6 I once worked with a cooperating teacher in an urban district to arrange a day trip to an environmental center for her AP biology class. We had funding for the buses, but the district office declined the trip request anyway because students would be in close proximity to a lake. Given the spate of bad publicity over the recent death of a student in a school pool, we were told that no field trips involving water would be approved. Our argument that the biology students would be walking in a stream collecting macroinvertebrates—and not going in the lake—were not persuasive.

7   Aside perhaps from just having students view a live webcam showing an image from a zoo, natural habitat, or a science laboratory. This is an excellent use of instructional technology for data collection, but students will never consider it to be a field trip.

8   I usually tried to get coffee and breakfast for the chaperones, and whenever possible, a quiet room where they can gather in the morning. And afterwards, thank you notes.

9   One other thing I discovered about field trips is that a great time to take them is during the last waning days of school before summer. These days are often a little surreal in high schools, because both grades and attendance have been submitted, and the regular school patterns seem suspended even in the most organized schools. While many students simply stay home, there are always a few students in the building, and this creates an opportunity for doing something that might not be possible earlier in the year. My last year in Trenton, with the help of my principal, I created a "hiking club" for the purposes of just one field trip, and took any kid in the school who wanted to go. I found some funding to pay for the bus and lunch, and we ended up with about 15 students and teachers who wanted to hike to the top of Mount Tammany to see the Delaware Water Gap. We did it all in one day.

10 I have done this trip multiple times, but for a few years we were able to fund the trip for all of the school's physics students through equalization aid provided by the state. As my students walked around the park in groups without chaperones—they were high school seniors after all—they congregated by benches and filled out their packets, the same way that the kids from the wealthier schools were doing. More than a few students told me that for once they did not feel like they were getting a second-class education. Any time someone tells me that money does not matter in education, I think about how it mattered a great deal for my physics students on that trip.

11 In fact, for a brief period in the 1970s, all pre-service teachers in the state of New Jersey were expected to do a practicum week at the New Jersey School of Conservation as a component of their environmental education.

10

"BEFORE TODAY I WAS AFRAID OF TREES"

Rethinking Nature Deficit Disorder in Diverse Classrooms

The last week of February turned out to be the peak of the maple-sugaring season that winter, and an inch of snow remained on the ground as the juniors in my chemistry class disembarked from the bus. Kevin, our guide, met us with empty buckets, and he talked about the trees as we took a short walk around. The students ran their hands over the bark of the oaks, beeches, and maples with an uncharacteristic quietness as our guide talked about the different types of trees in Cadwalader Park.

For the moment, it was possible to imagine that we were somewhere other than urban central New Jersey. To many of my students it was a revelation that we were not actually standing in a natural forest, but in a place where each of the towering trees had been purposefully planted by hand decades ago. Their questions led to a discussion about how trees in urban environments not only looked nice, but actually helped clean the air and lower energy costs by reducing the amount of sunlight absorbed by city surfaces on hot days.

When Kevin pointed out holes in one tree made from yellow-bellied sapsuckers, one group of boys began racing from tree to tree, seeing who could be the first to find and run their fingers over undiscovered sapsucker holes. A group of girls raised their eyes to the treetops, looking for the birds. Kevin held up the metal spout and asked if anyone would like to hammer in the first tap.

"Ain't it gonna hurt the tree?" came the response from one of my more solemn students. Kevin assured him that it would not. We tapped two trees that day, and everyone who wanted a turn hammering got one. When the first bucket was finally hung from the tap, the students were clearly less than impressed with the leisurely *drip, drip, drip* of the watery tree sap. He explained that the buckets would fill over the next few days, and he promised to bring them to us at school.

A Surprising Confession

We thanked Kevin and boarded our bus, and returned to school shortly before the end of the 80-minute block period. Back in the classroom, one of my African American students pulled me aside, saying, "I have to tell you something." At the beginning of the semester in January, she had loudly proclaimed in front of the whole class that she did not like science. Though she dutifully completed her chemistry assignments, little in science class had seemed to hold meaning for her. When she pulled me aside, I fully admit that I was hoping for one of those minor teaching vindications, the kind of small victory that keeps weather-beaten teachers in urban schools coming back year after year. What she said, however, was much more profound.

Out of earshot from the students congregating by the door, she said, "Before today, I was afraid of trees." This was not the sort of thing I expected a popular high school junior—or anyone else for that matter—to say, so I asked her to explain. She laughed and with a shrug said, "I mean, like I was always afraid of them! They're big and scary, and their bark is all rough-looking." She went on to describe how nature and outdoors things in general had always seemed somehow dangerous to her. In thinking about what ideas my own students might have had about maple syrup-making, the idea that some students might have a fear of trees had genuinely never occurred to me. I have looked over state and national science standards carefully since then, and none of them include anything about making students comfortable around trees. Yet there it was as an unintended and valuable outcome of the trip.

Diagnosing Nature Deficit Disorder

Science teachers in urban schools often serve students whose experiences with the natural environment are more visibly constrained by human factors than their suburban or rural counterparts. At the same time, parents and teachers nationwide have been contending with an increase in sedentary indoor activities that have affected youth (and frankly, adults as well) of every demographic. When coupled with the shrinking opportunities many children have for experiencing nature in an unbounded form, these factors can lead to a lack of familiarity with the fundamental features of ecology and the natural world.[1] Journalist Richard Louv has called the resulting situation "nature deficit disorder," a term that has resonated strongly with the environmental education community.[2]

Yet those with an understanding of the history of multicultural education have good reason to be suspicious of any terminology that causes teachers to view specific students from a "deficit" perspective. Though Louv is careful to describe the deficit as applying to children's experiences with the natural world, like many diagnostic labels it can easily become affixed to students themselves. Historically, deficit language like the term "at-risk" has been used to marginalize students already struggling for success in schools.[3] Rather than explore options that seek to build upon students' strengths, experiences, and prior understandings of the world, notions of cultural deprivation or deficiency have been used to explain away the failures of teachers to be effective in teaching such students.[4]

Environmental Education as Consciousness-raising

Three related goals usually frame most environmental education efforts. The first is to foster and sustain a love of nature. The second is to gain a scientific understanding of the environment, with knowledge of the factors, processes, and interrelationships that describe and explain the living world. The last is to help students make intelligent and informed choices in their lives. All are important, but depending on the school and the teacher, they may be prioritized differently.

In schools such as mine where students experienced marginalization and oppression, these three goals may also have served the purpose of what Paolo Freire calls *conscientization* (or in current parlance, being "woke.").[5] One need only to look to historical figures such as John Muir or Rachael Carson, or the modern-day coalition of climate change activists to see what conscientization looks like in an environmental sense. In his descriptions of the "criminalization of natural play," Richard Louv also clearly frames the public and private restrictions on children's experiences with nature as a form of oppression, and his work serves as a call to action.

Though I was teaching a chemistry course, there were many days when a passerby might have looked into my classroom and guessed that I was teaching an algebra, literature, or environmental science class instead. Administrators are fond of saying—particularly around testing season in the spring—that *every* teacher teaches reading, and *every* teacher teaches math. I argue that all teachers must be environmental educators as well. This is especially important for science teachers because fundamental ideas in biology, chemistry, physics, and earth science knowledge are crucial in making sense of pressing environmental issues such as climate change, industrial pollution, radioactive waste, food safety, and the destruction and alteration of habitats. In a high school chemistry class, being able to connect matters of environmental justice to chemistry is dependent upon students' ability to recognize their personal connections to these issues at all. This is why the idea of nature deficit disorder carries weight among many environmental educators; it offers a convincing explanation for a perceived lack of personal connections between students and environmental issues.

As a chemistry teacher in an urban school, I often strayed beyond the traditional sequence of topics in the discipline, which usually follow a predictable progression from properties of matter, through atomic theory and bonding, and finish somewhere around chemical reactions and electron configurations to bonding to acids and bases. Some chemistry curricula provide connections to environmental issues, and these serve as valuable resources for teaching topics like water quality, petrochemicals, and nuclear energy.[6] There are countless possible links between chemistry and environmental justice, but like any curriculum, how far these go depends on the teacher.

For example, in my chemistry class that year my students examined the suitability of Yucca Mountain as a repository for nuclear waste as part of our nuclear chemistry unit. In a visit to the radiation laboratory in the hospital across the street from our school, technicians showed the students exactly how the instruments worked, and described the differences between the radioactive isotopes they used for scans (like technetium-99m, with a half-life of 6 hours) and ones used in nuclear power generation (such as plutonium-239, with a half-life of 24,000 years). Later during a lesson on ions, we watched clips from the movie *Erin Brockovich* as a catalyst for discussion for both environmental justice and the electron configuration of hexavalent chromium (Cr^{+6}).

Tapping into Community Resources

Kevin Kopp has been a well-known environmental educator in the central New Jersey area for years, offering workshops and educational programs for classes for a range of students. As a busy high school science teacher in Trenton, I had ignored his program announcements for many months because many of the activities seemed geared to younger students, even though they were advertised as appropriate for K-12. One of his e-mails finally caught my attention. It read:

> Bring your class to Cadwalader Park and learn about one of the true wonders of nature. This is a special program on maple sugaring and making maple syrup. Through stories and hands-on activities, students will learn about the legends, history and modern practices of making maple syrup. Each group will tap a tree, collect sap, and taste some Cadwalader Park maple syrup.

The idea that trees in our city could produce maple syrup was too good to pass up. Not only would this trip to Cadwalader Park—a place that had been publicized in recent years more as a crime scene than for its environmental features—provide students with a solid connection between food, chemistry, and the environment, it was also a way to develop their critical consciousness around issues of natural resources. Why was something like maple syrup, which could be gathered from trees in their neighborhoods, only a trace ingredient in the commercially produced packages of syrup that came with school breakfast? Pushing further, we could also ask why some people get to control where food comes from at all. If food exists naturally in places in the world, like cod in the Atlantic or raspberry vines on the sunny edge of a park, what responsibility does that place upon the rest of us to ensure a world that sustains these and other resources for current and future generations? *Not* thinking about these issues is an element of Louv's nature deficit disorder description, but we can just as well consider it a form of oppression imposed by the modern world. My thinking was that the act of seeing their own city differently could open up possibilities of action for my students.

Though I had not planned on teaching solutions and molarity for another two months, it proved simple enough to develop an appropriate lesson on concentration that related to the task of boiling down syrup. My principal quickly approved the trip, and it did not hurt that it would all take place within a single 80-minute block and required only one bus.

Kevin and I constructed a minimalist plan for the trip over email, agreeing to the approach of simply tapping the trees and telling stories along the way. He would focus on the history and process of maple sugaring, and I would inject science ideas into the narrative wherever appropriate. In preparation, I found myself reading widely about the science of maple sap, and reconsidering some of my own ideas about how it was produced. I unexpectedly had to review most of the tree biology I had ever learned.

Kitchen Chemistry

The week after the trip, Kevin delivered two full five-gallon buckets to our class. According to our plan, one was full of the maple sap and the other was just water. We set students the challenge of identifying each without tasting, and within a short time, lab groups were scribbling possible procedures in their notebooks. Though one of the liquids was clear and the other was cloudy I informed them that this was insufficient evidence. After all, these buckets of liquid had been sitting outside for a few days. This and the fact that our chemistry lab equipment was not "food grade" was the reason I ruled out (for the moment) tasting the unpasteurized liquids.

Once I had approved their procedures for safety and feasibility, I permitted my students to proceed with their ideas for testing the two liquids. Though I had hoped that at least one group would measure the densities of the two liquids, as soon as the first lab group—wearing safety goggles—started a Bunsen burner with an evaporating dish, the rest of the class took the hint and quickly followed suit. Before the end of the period, many of the dishes contained brown syrup in the bottom. There was still some skepticism on the part of the students that this was actually the same stuff they would put on waffles—especially because I would not let them taste it, so the next week's activity was designed to make this idea more plausible.

I brought in some saucepans from home, careful to keep the food preparation area in the back of the room clean, safe, and free of any chemistry lab equipment that could potentially contaminate the syrup. I decided to boil down the sap with the electric hotplates, but scorched my first test batch during homeroom, to the slight annoyance of the other teachers in my area of the building who had to endure the burnt smell for the rest of the day. I asked student volunteers from my morning physics classes to help me by stirring the sap and adding more whenever the mixture started to get too concentrated. By the time my chemistry class arrived in the afternoon, I had about 50 ml of Cadwalader Park syrup ready, and together we started another batch boiling down.

Though a formal study of chemical reactions was still weeks away, there would hardly be a more opportune time to discuss the chemistry of cooking. I did a brief demonstration of the differences between baking soda and baking powder, showing how each needed an acid in an aqueous solution in order to release the carbon dioxide. We examined the ingredients in a box of store-bought mix, and using a griddle from home, I whipped up a batch of pancakes, cutting them open to point out the role of the carbon dioxide in the rising of the batter as it cooked.[7] In order not to break my own rules about food in the lab, we remained in the front half of the classroom as I passed out paper plates and plastic forks, and not a single student passed on the opportunity to eat pancakes with syrup they had literally traced to its roots. The student who had overcome her fear of trees could not contain her enthusiasm, "Look at him, he all up there cooking pancakes like it ain't nothin'!"

Later that week, a number of my students worked together to compose an e-mail to Kevin. It read:

> Dear Mr. Kopp,
> This is Mr. Larkin's class. Bucket #1 = water, Bucket #2 = sap. We realized this after scientifically heating the evaporating dishes. After around 5 to 10 minutes the water began to evaporate from both dishes. Soon dish #2 began to turn a brownish color, while dish #1 just evaporated until nothing was left. When we first examined the contents of container 1 & 2, container #2 had a cloudy color which differed from container #1. The sense of smell around the dishes was also different.
> Thank you for your time,
> Luis, Muhammad, Miguel, Kendra, Brandon, Jessica, Sasha, and the rest of our period 6/7 Chemistry class

Cultivating a Naturalist Intelligence vs. Remediating Deficiency

When I originally proposed the idea for the trip to my students in the first week of the new semester, they were eager to do something out of the ordinary, though some expressed doubts that we would really be doing chemistry. It was not unusual in their experience to go on "fun" field trips with the loosest of ties to any learning goals. Certainly, I had seen well-meaning teachers organize such trips, but I also suspected that some were rooted in deficit notions about experiences—often suburban in character—teachers felt that students needed in order to be considered educated. Therefore, I was determined to build high academic expectations into the trip. The fact that we could extend our learning about chemistry into the community, and specifically the outdoors, was an implicit part of my motivation, as was the opportunity to develop students' critical consciousness around issues of food production.

My student's admission about overcoming her fear of trees reminded me that some outcomes will always be unplanned, but it is possible that others would view her understanding of nature as deficient, or even pathological. Undoubtedly, her prior ideas about trees were influenced by the broad societal forces described by Louv that teach children to avoid having direct experiences with nature. Though Louv's critique is meant to apply widely to modern childhood, it is also true that those most likely to be constructed as "deficient" are those living in urban environments. Given the residential demographics of the U.S., it is also true that these children are also more likely than not to be of African American and Latino/a backgrounds. Louv has given voice to a vitally important idea, but his deficit language may be ultimately harmful to those students who could perhaps benefit from its implications the most. What's an urban environmental educator to do?

In a revision to his original list of multiple intelligences, Howard Gardner added the notion of a *naturalist intelligence* and described it as the intelligence that "enables human beings to recognize, categorize and draw upon certain features of the environment."[8] Rather than viewing a student's limited understanding of the natural world as a deficit to be remediated, Gardner's work suggests that student ideas and experiences are a starting point for developing this intelligence. Yet doing so entails more than just letting students loose in nature—though that is not always a bad idea. As teachers, we need to understand not only our students' prior knowledge about the natural world, but also the ways in which they think about and experience it.

I once observed a lesson in an urban middle school where a white teacher from a suburban background assigned homework to her students (who were all African American), in which they were to go outside and look at the sky every night in order to collect data on the phases of the moon. Sitting in the back of the room, I heard one young girl say to her friend that she could not do the assignment because she was forbidden to go outside at night where she lived. While such a situation might be considered as one more example of how "nature deficit disorder" has severed students' connections with the natural world, a different perspective might illustrate this restriction as a rational parental response to living in a dangerous neighborhood. Had the teacher known more about her students' lives, she could have intentionally structured the activity differently to accommodate their realities, perhaps by anticipating times when moon observations could be made during daylight hours. Doing so would have built upon the opportunities students actually had for engaging with the natural world, rather than relying on assumptions the teacher had constructed that were based on her own life experiences.

It is equally important however, that urban educators do not assume that students in their schools have minimal experience with the natural world. Some students and their families may be seasonal farm workers with a rich knowledge of agriculture. Others, such as the Hmong students I taught in Wisconsin, regularly enjoy hunting in the forests of the upper Midwest, leveraging their rich cultural traditions regarding the natural world toward new understandings of an ecosystem quite different from the hills of Southeast Asia.[9]

Rather than viewing students as having "nature deficit disorder," teachers can develop both the naturalist intelligence and the critical consciousness of students by building on the ways they actually do experience the world. Educators can extend Louv's ideas into formal science classrooms (without the deficit language baggage) by seeking to cultivate more opportunities for natural experiences, rather than simply compensating for their absence. The environmental knowledge used by a student to ride the subway system across town to school in New York City is quite different in character from that of the suburban New Jersey youth who plays soccer every Saturday on a grassy field, and different also from that used by the teenager in rural Pennsylvania who plants corn and milks cows. Yet all are forms of environmental knowledge that hold opportunities for teachers to meet students where they are in their thinking about the connections between the human-influenced environment and the natural world. Making these connections also gives science teachers a good reason to make pancakes and syrup in chemistry class.

Notes

1 My sister Julia tells a story about one of her middle school students in the Bronx happening upon a construction site with her friends and watching through the fence in fascination as the workers tore up the asphalt in order to excavate the ground underneath. Though this student had been one of the highest achievers in the class, the idea that there was soil under the slabs of the city was a revelation to her and many of her classmates.

2 Louv's (2005) work covers other important and related topics as well, including the criminalization of play in nature that occurs when children are forbidden from engaging in activities (like tree-climbing) that humans are literally built to do.

3 In the 1990s, there was a push to discourage the use of this label (e.g. Cuban, 1989; Maimon, 1999), but it was largely unsuccessful, and "at-risk" remains a common term in public education discourse today (Ladson-Billings, 2000). Those critiquing its continued use commonly place the term in scare quotes or use person-first language in order to mark its problematic nature (e.g. Martin & Beese, 2017).

4 Such impoverished folk theories of student achievement are unfortunately still in existence, but modern research and scholarship emphasizes the influence of the teacher as a significant factor in student learning (e.g. Haberman, Gillette, & Hill, 2018; Hattie, 2009; MET project, 2012; Villegas & Lucas, 2002).

5 To Freire (1970), conscientization was, "learning to perceive social, political and economic contradictions, and to take action against the oppressive elements of reality," (p. 35).

6 The Chemistry in the Community (ChemCom) materials published by the American Chemical Society (2012) are particularly good at highlighting the linkages between environmental science and chemistry.

7 From the perspective of a decade later, I regret all of the opportunities for puzzling phenomena that I missed. I could have taken time later to have students try to figure

out why the pancakes had bubbles in them, why they thought the syrup turned brown, etc. Honestly, I think my main concern at that point was not burning anything else.

8 (Gardner, 1999, p. 48).

9 There is a wonderful example of leveraging such insights in the ethnographic interviews conducted by teachers in the Funds of Knowledge project (González, Moll, & Amanti, 2005), when teachers in a school in Tucson, Arizona unexpectedly learned that many of their English language learner students possessed a deep knowledge about horses. Teacher/researcher Cathy Amani writes: "Once it became clear to me that a substantial portion of my class had background knowledge and experiences relating to horses, and once I decided to implement a module on this topic, I began collecting resources such as books and videos, and contacting guest speakers, including my students' parents." (p. 135).

PART III
Science Teacher Learning

11

OBSERVING CANDLES AND CLASSROOMS

Learning from Other Teachers by Withholding Judgment

One of the key insights that has been gleaned from the past few centuries with regard to doing science can be summed up by the phrase, "If I am wrong, how would I know?" Asking this question regularly is not just a healthy practice for scientists, but a good habit for anyone who endeavors to make sense of world in a rational way. Raising this question in public is also an effective way to trouble the waters when people are excessively sure of themselves.[1]

When the pre-service teachers with whom I work are sent out to schools to observe teachers, their first impressions about what they see often turn out to be misleading. This can also happen to teachers, parents, administrators, instructional coaches, university faculty, or anyone else who finds themselves visiting a classroom. Even though being an outside observer can offer a fresh perspective for keen insights, it is easy for someone who is less familiar with the students, teachers, or school setting to draw mistaken conclusions simply out of a shortage of information. Clearly understanding what we observe in classrooms is difficult because we humans tend to let our emotions and values influence our explanations. How something makes us feel can affect what we think we see, and it is not always so easy to separate our observations, interpretations, and judgments from one another.

★★★

There is a wonderfully simple science activity with a pedigree going back at least as far as Michael Faraday's lectures at the Royal Institution in London in the mid-1800s, in which students light a candle, drip a bit of the wax onto the table to hold it firmly, and then are told to make as many observations as possible in a certain amount of time without touching the candle again.[2] When working with high-school students, I have occasionally stretched this activity past the half-hour mark, with some groups making over a hundred observations. Students then read their lists aloud out to see who has the greatest number of unique observations not recorded by other groups.

Then comes the reveal, which is a brief lecture on the distinction between observation and inference. *Observations* are what we can perceive with our senses, or at least with instruments that help us extend the range and sensitivity of our senses (e.g. microscopes, thermometers, pH meters, mass spectrometers, etc.). An observation is statement of a fact, one upon which other human observers would concur.[3] However, an observation becomes an *inference* when prior knowledge has been drawn upon to describe something beyond our senses, or assumptions have been made about what is actually known in a given situation, or reasoning leads to a tentative conclusion. For example, the first few items on a student's list of observations may read as follows:

1.) The candle is white.
2.) Wax is dripping down the side.
3.) The candle smells like pine trees and cinnamon.
4.) The flame is yellow on the bottom and blue on top.
5.) The candle is burning oxygen from the air.
6.) There is a little liquid puddle of wax at the top.

The first four items on the list would probably meet with broad agreement as statements of fact, though perhaps an observer with color-blindness might describe the flame differently, or the smell reference might differ based on students' experiences.[4] That the candle is burning oxygen, however, is not something observable, and must be inferred from other sources—perhaps from a previous encounter with an explanation for combustion. And while everyone might agree upon the existence of a little puddle on the top of the candle, identifying it as wax goes one step beyond what can be figured out from observation alone.[5]

This activity can be a very good exercise to help observers learn to distinguish between fact and inference, and I highly recommend its use. However, as soon as our gaze turns from candles to classrooms, things get a bit more difficult.

★★★

I have a five-minute video clip that I regularly show to my undergraduate and graduate students to illuminate the differences between observation, interpretation, and judgment.[6] Usually I ask my students to write down what they notice, but sometimes I also ask for comments on what they find familiar and unfamiliar in comparison with their own schooling, just as a way to get started.

The clip begins with a scene of an elongated science classroom with purple accented walls on the short sides, a long row of windows in the back, and a series of whiteboards, blackboards, and bulletin boards across the front. A large amount of space is taken up by a teacher desk and a demonstration table, leaving the remaining area for about 36 students to be packed behind tightly arranged lab tables in the center. The room setup leaves very little space for students to move, but otherwise it appears to be a typical classroom.

The students are in the sixth grade and are chatting loudly as the class begins. They all appear to be African American. The teacher, Mr. M., greets the class with a faint "Okay class, I need quiet to get started." Half of the class waits silently, looking up front, but the other half keeps talking, even after a second plea for their silence and attention. Suddenly a child in the front row yells, "Show him the respect you'd show your momma!" This brings the noise level of the class down significantly.

As the students settle down, the teacher begins telling a story about an experiment done in the 1700s to try to test a common theory at the time about the apparent creation of animals under the proper conditions. He does not use the term "spontaneous generation," with the students, but describes this historical idea in everyday language instead.[7] While he is talking, the children's voices are audible as a low murmur. At the edges of room, three other adults are tending to students. One is in the back of the room having a hushed conversation with a girl in the last row, another in the front corner is seated with three students surrounding her, and the third is shepherding latecomers from the side lab tables to their seats. Even as the room settles, it remains a hive of activity with many potential distractions.

The teacher shows some slides, asks a couple of questions, and persuades a few individual students to answer. Some are clearly not happy about being called upon to participate. The clip ends as Mr. M. continues having his discussion with the class one student at a time, while the sound of talking in the classroom grows louder. To many observers, it is difficult to make sense of the scene because what unfolds is not clear cut or framed in any way. It is a problem space without clear definition of the problem.[8] The reasons why relate to the nature of the difficulty in disentangling the differences between observation, interpretation, and judgment.

When trying to make sense of the goings-on in any social situation, the small inferences we make tend to give way to broader *interpretations* of human behavior. These interpretations have a few key features. First is that any interpretation is an attempt to make meaning out of what has been observed. Second, interpretations depend on making assumptions, inferences, or guesses about what was unseen, or by suggesting connections between events, all of which depend upon the ways in which we organize and retrieve our prior knowledge. Lastly, interpretations are a part of the essential human struggle to make sense of the world, and our brains do this by constructing stories.[9] Of course, the stories we like best are often the ones that fit comfortably within our existing narratives about the world.

There is a good argument from a psychological perspective that what we call observation is already a form of interpretation.[10] An example of sensory perception might go something like this: "I see a small ball. It appears to be growing in size, getting bigger every moment. Now my nose hurts quite a bit and I cannot see the ball." The statement "I got hit in the nose by a ball" is therefore an interpretation of this sensory information. However, describing this as being hit in the nose by a ball is the description most people who witnessed the event would give.

It is worth noting that culture acts as a set of filters through which such interpretation happens, and goes on to influence judgments. For example, growing up in primarily White middle-class schools, my experience was that when someone needed to blow their nose, they got a tissue, blew their nose and threw the used tissue away in the garbage. If someone did those things in that order, it could reasonably be described as blowing his or her nose. However, later when I was a teacher in an urban school with a mostly African American population, I noticed that the concept of blowing one's nose entailed a degree of privacy I had not previously experienced. Students would ask for a tissue, walk out the door into the hallway for a moment, sometimes even shutting the door, and then discreetly disposing of the tissue before returning to their seat.

Therefore, what it meant to "blow your nose" was different in each school, even when people used the same words. When a student asked to blow her nose in my urban classroom, she was really asking permission to leave the classroom momentarily. A teacher (or an observer) unaware of this might interpret the student's exit from the classroom as a discipline issue of sorts, and form judgments that flowed from this view. Unfortunately, I learned this the hard way, once when I called out a student for trying to sneak out of my class, when all she was trying to do was blow her nose in private.

★★★

When I show the video of Mr. M.'s sixth-grade science classroom, a typical sample of my students' observations might include the following:

1) The room is very cramped.
2) There are three other adults in the room
3) The students are disrespectful.
4) The teacher tried to make the lesson interesting by asking if it was possible to have a "recipe for making rats."
5) This teacher is terrible (or awesome).
6) The teacher should have waited until students were quiet.

The first two are indeed observations, while the third and fourth draw upon other information to form an interpretation. But the last two statements are neither, and are better described as *judgments* because they are opinions driven by a specific interpretation of events. Claiming that a teacher is awesome or terrible—even if informed by observations, interpretations, and careful deliberation—reflects the values of the observer about what constitutes good teaching. Similarly, the critique that the teacher should have waited indicates an implicit judgment that the course of action by the teacher was incorrect. Neither has explanatory power, and both say more about the observer than the observed.[11]

We live in a culture that gives the idea of judgment significant currency; there is even an entire television genre dedicated to the judging of singing, dancing and courtship performances. Social media is awash with "likes," and decades of applied marketing psychology have conditioned us to express our preferences with purchases and to identify with brands in order to be judged positively by others. If we were fish, this would be the water in which we swim, invisible yet all around us.

Making judgments in a classroom situation, particularly as an outside observer, is fraught with peril because judgments obstruct our ability to understand what is happening by assigning undue weight to interpretations that may not be correct. For example, an observer who decides that Mr. M is not a good teacher because the students are disrespectful may be operating from a particular vision of what "respectful" students look and act like. It is also possible that an observer's interpretation of "respect" in the video is influenced by the crowded conditions of the room environment, the age of the students, or the racial makeup of the class, rather than by the behavior of the actual students themselves or whether they demonstrate an improved understanding of designing and carrying out an experiment.

Not only that, but it is in the very nature of the situation that a classroom observer has incomplete information. Once, when I was conducting an observation in a 7th grade life science class, I watched with astonishment as the student teacher systematically ignored a student in a wheelchair for the entire period. There was an aide in the class however, who sat next to the student and appeared to work closely with her. By the end of the period I was left quite disappointed, concluding that the student teacher was simply ignoring our program's efforts to foster inclusive practices, and was taking advantage of the fact that she could basically outsource the teaching of her student with disabilities to someone else. I formed some severe judgments and prepared myself to share them in our post-observation conference. We sat down in the school library afterward, and when I started the conference by asking her opinion on how the lesson went, she burst into tears. Apparently, the principal had met with and her cooperating teacher that morning to let them know that the aide was being fired that afternoon, and he instructed them not to interact with him—"Just get through the day," he had told them. She had not been able to tell me because the aide was already in the classroom when I arrived.

★★★

After I show the video and everyone makes their lists of observations, I follow the same sequence of steps that I described in the candle activity. However, once we have distinguished between observation and interpretation, I have students scan their lists again to look for value-laden language and critiques that could reasonably be considered judgments. At this point, I typically meet some (respectful) resistance. There is almost always at least one exasperated student who asks if I am suggesting that they should refrain from making any judgments at all.

Yes, I tell them. That is exactly what I am saying.

Consciously resisting judgments or critiques in such situations is difficult, but it is also absolutely necessary because judgments get in the way of figuring out what is going on. Remaining non-judgmental also helps observers avoid the tangle of complex feelings that inevitably occur when an observer's judgment is made public, either inadvertently or intentionally. Even when the critique is positive, it is rare for an unrequested opinion to be gratefully received.

I always tell my students to try to develop more than one idea to explain what they see in any given classroom, and encourage them to assign a probability to each tentative explanation. When the world is viewed from multiple perspectives, it may be the case that more than one truth exists at any given time, so these probabilities need not sum to 100%.

In the case of Mr. M.'s classroom in the video, the interpretation that the students are disrespectful of the teacher does have some probability of being true. Yet, observers could look for clues in the video to decide if student talking continues because they are engaged in talking about the science. We can look for evidence of established routines, and cues that communicate to the students what they should be doing while the teacher is talking. Such an investigation often leads to other possible explanations for the students' behavior.

Perhaps it is just before lunchtime and the students are hungry [moderate probability]. Maybe there was a fight in the hall before the class started, and the students are still overexcited from the spectacle [low probability]. Perhaps the teacher has lost the trust of students somehow and the students' behavior is the result [low probability], or the teacher's own nervousness signals to the students that the class period will be disorganized [high probability]. It could be that the sheer density of human beings confined to such a small space makes it difficult to focus [very high probability]. Finally, there is always the possibility that it is the teacher's first day in front of these students, and he has yet to build any kind of relationship with them [very low probability, but quite true in the case of this video clip].

Our explanations can expand to include questions whose answers might help us refine our interpretations, such as: Why does the adult in the corner only work with three students? How strong is the teacher in his knowledge of the topic? How hungry are the students? What did the students expect to be doing in class? What are the normal class routines?

We may also include factors outside the classroom as well, to help avoid what social psychologists call the *fundamental attribution error*, that is, crediting characteristics to individual behavior that are really a consequence of the context.[12] What role does the room setup play in the students' behavior? Is this a magnet school? How were the teachers prepared? What is the workload of the teachers like? Why is this classroom monoracial? Might residential segregation play a role here in the class size? The trick is to attend to our emotions and gut instincts as we develop a range of interpretations, while avoiding the temptation to make judgments and critiques.

Developing multiple interpretations gets one in the habit of framing events through different lenses, in order to consider the possible range of interpretations that can result. In formal teacher evaluations, administrators and supervisors often separate their description of the events of a class from the interpretations, judgments, and suggestions for improvement. This is a learned skill that takes great practice, and is much harder to do than it seems. To do it well often requires gathering more evidence from the teacher after the fact—usually in a time and place removed from the rough and tumble of the classroom—so that information about unseen influences can be incorporated into the final evaluation.[13] From an administrative perspective, it is both appropriate and necessary for an evaluator to make judgments about the teaching and decide on the best way to provide feedback to the teacher once these interpretations have been made. Other observers who are *not* responsible for providing evaluative feedback may find that it is more worthwhile generating new questions to ask, rather than judgments to render.

Therefore, to summarize the above into a set of guidelines for classroom observations:

- Record the facts of what is happening. I suggest three columns—one each for time, teacher actions, and student actions. For my own organization, I like to draw a bold line to indicate when a new section or activity of the lesson is apparent.
- Develop multiple interpretations of what might explain those observations, particularly when students respond unexpectedly to the actions of the teacher or when other critical incidents occur. Assign each possible explanation a probability of being correct (e.g. likely, very likely, not likely, etc.).
- Consider what information might help refine those explanations. Prepare questions that can be asked later if possible, all the while resisting the temptation to pass judgment.

In fact, I would argue that it is wise for teachers at all times to resist making judgments, at least until doing so is needed to decide on a course of action. That is when making judgments becomes absolutely essential, especially when making decisions under conditions of uncertainty.[14]

I was trained as a physicist, so I think of this in terms of superpositioned waves states—i.e. Schrödinger's cat is both alive and dead inside the box—for the various interpretations of what is going on in any given situation. I can hold all of those interpretations at once in my mind as possibilities, some more probable than others. Then, when I need to make a decision (and the box with the cat is opened!), all of the wave functions collapse into a single observed state that represents the best interpretation I can make in that moment. That interpretation then influences the judgment call I need to make, which then drives my decision-making.

So, if I am sitting in the back of a student teacher's classroom watching an eleventh-grader next to me avoid doing anything related to the lesson for ten minutes, I can usually come up with five or six different theories as to what may be going on. Maybe she's tired, sick, or having a bad day. Maybe she's far ahead of the rest of the class and bored out of her mind. Maybe she and the teacher do not get along. Maybe she does not see what this topic has to do with her life. Maybe she needs accommodations that she is not receiving. There are lots of possibilities available for interpreting her behavior, and I leave them all open. However, when she suddenly becomes aware of my existence and turns to ask if I have a pencil, I have to cast my lot with one explanation—that her disengagement was a result of being unprepared for class, and maybe she was even a little embarrassed—in order to decide how to respond.[15]

We are wrong a great deal of the time in classroom observations because our information is almost always incomplete, yet we retain the capacity to test our hypotheses about the world by seeking disconfirming evidence. As teachers, the ability to align this type of thoughtful reflection with our professional goals helps us grow. By asking, "If I am wrong, how would I know?" just like scientists do, we are led to seek out the sources of evidence that might tell us if our theories are on the wrong track. Only then does it become more likely that we will be less wrong over time.

Notes

1 Questions such as, "If you were wrong about (vaccines causing autism/the earth being six thousand years old/the genetic superiority of people with white skin), how would you know?" are important to pose, if for no other reason than that they offer a potential entry point into rationality.
2 I first read this volume (Faraday, 1938) as a new teacher, and was startled that a lecture nearly 150 years old could seem so relevant.
3 Obviously, I am not referring to events that concern either relativity or quantum mechanics in these situations.
4 For example, a student with limited experience with pine trees might say it smelled like their grandmother's house.
5 That puddle might not even be wax! Little puddles form on the outside of cold soda cans after they come out of a vending machine, but we do not usually suppose that they are drops of liquid aluminum.
6 The video was shared with me by a student teacher who made the recording as an assignment for a university class and agreed to let me use it for teaching purposes. I have shown this scene to literally hundreds of undergraduate and graduate students, and found it to be a wonderful probe for eliciting people's ideas about good teaching.
7 In watching this clip, many observers fail to note the intentional move being made here by Mr. M in first representing complex concepts in everyday language so that students can understand the idea.

8 This is similar to the ill-formed way that real-world scientific problems often present themselves.

9 Bransford, Brown, & Cocking, 1999.

10 In philosophy, there is also a more ontological argument by Nietzsche about the existence of facts, represented in his famous claim that "there are no facts; only interpretations," but that is somewhat beyond the scope of the present discussion.

11 Note that in the candle example, judgment does not have an analog, unless someone says, "I enjoy the way the candle makes the room smell like pine needles and cinnamon."

12 Educational researcher Mary Kennedy (2010) has written at length about the ways in which the fundamental attribution error operates in assessments of teacher quality.

13 Of course, this is much more difficult to do with a video clip as compared to a live observation.

14 And as Nobel Prize-winning psychologist Daniel Kahneman (2011) notes in his monumental work, *Thinking, Fast and Slow*, even then we can be quite wrong.

15 I always have an extra pencil.

12

MENTORING NEW SCIENCE TEACHERS

Novices Get Better When We Support Them with Good Feedback

I recently visited a student teacher at the end of his first month of full-time student teaching in an urban magnet school, and I had high hopes for him in his new placement.[1] I had watched him struggle with teaching science to 6th graders during his initial practicum and was looking forward to seeing him teach a lesson in physics, his college major and area of teacher certification. He had assured me that a high school physics class was where he belonged, given his experience as an electrical engineer in a previous career.

When I arrived at his room a few minutes before class, he had just stepped out into the hall while his cooperating teacher handled the ten-minute advisory period. His appearance reminded me of a wrestler leaving the ring, and the way he mopped the sweat off his forehead and arched his back against the lockers communicated a deep exhaustion. He caught his breath and greeted me, and when I asked him how it was going, he simply said, "This is really hard."

As I watched him teach that afternoon, I understood completely. It was the last day of the marking period, and he seemed barraged by students with last-minute work all throughout the hour. Furthermore, his students had not understood the previous day's lab on heat capacity, and his patient explanations and expertly formatted slides did not seem to be helping much. A demonstration in which he tried to boil water in a bell jar at room temperature completely failed to work, even after his cooperating teacher stepped in to help. After 10 minutes, they both admitted defeat and moved on with the lesson. I had hoped we could chat after class, but as soon as the bell rang, he was swamped at the front desk by students jockeying for his time and attention. We only managed a distant wave, with an implicit promise to catch up later. As I returned over the course of the semester, the strain of student teaching was never far from the surface, even as he continued to find joy in teaching a subject he loved.

For more than a decade, I have spent time in science classrooms researching how people learn to teach science, and have come to deeply appreciate the role that cooperating teachers and mentors play in the process. Undoubtedly, cooperating teachers have ideas about how people learn to teach, and these ideas influence the types of support they offer to their student teachers. Yet, these ideas and personal theories do not always align with the emerging research on learning to teach, creating tensions and pressures on the very people they intend to help.

Here are some things we know: Learning to teach is stressful and is a time of intense personal transitions that often forces people to change who they think they are.[2] Novice teachers also come with their own ideas about teaching formed from their own experiences, and they often use their own schooling as a guide for best practice.[3] Their own experiences with inquiry inside and outside science classrooms greatly influences their likelihood of fostering inquiry in their own classrooms as teachers.[4] They may know they are supposed to address misconceptions, but then are not quite sure what to do with student ideas once they are out in the open.[5] Many are still learning the content, and most are struggling with both teaching equitably to all students and keeping pace with district curriculum guidelines.[6] We also know that novice science teachers usually try to enact the vision of good science teaching they encounter as they learn to teach, and messages about good science teaching can come from teacher education programs, colleagues, and mentors, as well as from the culture of the schools in which they work.[7]

In some cases, enacting this vision means adhering closely to particular resources and approaches that rely on following the guidelines of expert curriculum developers. For others, good science teaching may entail learning cycles with vibrant activities, lesson planning through "backward design," or reflective practices that weave social justice topics into every science unit. It is challenging for novice teachers to integrate their own ideas about good teaching with those of their teacher education programs and schools where they teach. Furthermore, enacting this vision of good science teaching in an actual classroom with actual students may be even more daunting. The mentoring that new teachers receive has significant consequences for how these challenges are addressed.

To aid in making such choices, I present here ten suggestions for mentoring novice teachers in high school science classes. These suggestions come from my own work in tracking prospective high school science teachers in different university-based teacher education programs. Though they are aimed primarily at cooperating teachers working in a mentoring relationship with full-time student teachers, there are now many ways to prepare science teachers that do not employ traditional student teaching experiences. Some novice teachers begin working immediately as a teacher of record, and receive infrequent mentoring, while others in teacher residency programs are among the most supported types of teacher learners in the history of teacher education. Yet even a teacher with a few years of experience can benefit from a mentoring relationship from an experienced master teacher, so even though I use the phrases "cooperating teacher" and "student teacher" below, my hope is that the suggestions are more broadly applicable to any other type mentor/mentee pairs.

1. Stay With Them in the Classroom.

During my research, I was surprised by how many cooperating teachers simply disappeared, thinking that they were doing their student teachers a favor. Science teachers tend to have prep rooms, and this can seem an attractive place to hide in order to give a student teacher more autonomy. Though well-intentioned, this practice denies student teachers the opportunity to receive ongoing feedback based on the cooperating teacher's professional knowledge and observations. By the end of student teaching, leaving them alone may be an appropriate strategy, but for the first few months, student teachers need formative feedback and logistical support even if they seem quite capable of doing things on their own. Student teachers have often reported to me that their need for feedback is more pressing than their desire for autonomy.

Many cooperating teachers are apprehensive about bruising the emerging professional egos of their student teachers, yet student teaching may be one of the few times in a teacher's career when they have the opportunity to learn hard truths about their teaching from a knowledgeable and caring colleague. Many student teachers genuinely want these conversations to occur. Little learning will take place if they hear that everything is "fine." The best mentors appear to practice compassionate confrontation, offering useful, timely feedback in manageable chunks so as not to seem overwhelming. Usually just addressing one or two major issues from each lesson is sufficient.

#2. Turn on Your Commentary Track.

Many movies on DVD have an option to turn on the director's commentary audio track, so the viewer can hear about what went into the making of the film, highlighting details that might otherwise be very difficult to perceive. Likewise, good cooperating teachers can keep a running commentary going for student teachers. This can help prevent student teachers from uncritical imitation, and focus their attention instead on the underlying goals of a particular practice. It is also a way to share hard-won practical wisdom. If a cooperating teacher organizes a lab activity in a certain way after tweaking it for years, talking through the reasons why can be very beneficial to a student teacher.

#3. Work With Your Student Teacher to Find Creative Outlets.

A common frustration among student teachers concerns the curricular constraints they feel upon entering their classrooms. Though this is often true in the case of undergraduates in their 20s, who continue to make up the majority of new teachers, older career-changers may feel this way too. Ready to spread their wings and fly, the last thing many wish to hear is that they will be following a carefully prepared common curriculum that their new colleagues have developed. Student teachers often have ideas about the creative lessons and activities they wish to do—some of which may even be required by their teacher education program— only to find that there is no space to implement their plans.

Student teachers often fail to realize that a curriculum does not teach itself. Simply having established learning goals and activities does not mean a lesson will just unfold automatically. Student teachers can be given the task of deciding exactly what they will say to introduce a lesson, elicit student ideas, run a discussion, review assignments, or organize class data from a lab activity, and can be encouraged to be creative in these tasks. Helping them find professional outlets for their creativity is a valuable way to channel their desire to show what they can do. This has the added benefit of focusing them on planning at the level of the specific discourse moves they intend to make, and may help nurture the collaborative skills they will need as teachers.

#4. Model How to Teach in a Constructivist Manner.

In far too many science classes, students still spend a great deal of time copying notes from the front of the room. Whether the delivery device is a chalkboard, screen, or electronic whiteboard, student teachers often think about teaching in terms of transmitting content to students rather than thinking about teaching as a way to help students build coherent structures of knowledge for themselves. This is particularly true in secondary science, where much of the content—especially as presented in textbooks—can seem sequential and indisputable.

Novices may be new to the notion that student ideas are the raw material of our work as teachers. One way to do this is to focus collective planning efforts on eliciting student ideas about science phenomena for the purpose of using those ideas in instruction. Student teachers can be encouraged to attend to student ideas and student thinking in general with assessment probes, journals, do-nows, demonstrations, think–pair–shares, and tasks that require the presentation of explanatory arguments from evidence.

Teaching this way also means tapping into students' ways of understanding and communicating about the world. Often, this entails taking into account the range of life experiences students bring to the task of learning, as well as leveraging student diversity as a resource to be tapped rather than an obstacle to be overcome. Novice teachers may appreciate suggestions on specific opportunities to study the students themselves and learn more about their lives, and will likely benefit from guidance on how to connect their science teaching to what they discover.

#5. Share Topic-specific Science Teaching Knowledge.

A master teacher might know six ways to teach the concept of density, but student teachers may just have one, and that one way may simply reflect how they learned it in school when they were younger. A pressing concern for novice teachers is the development of a repertoire of topic-specific practices, representations of the content, and knowledge about various approaches for teaching different topics. Cooperating teachers know a great deal about all of these, and even sharing strategies they themselves do not use will help their student teachers enrich their repertoire of what is possible in their own science teaching.

No science methods course can prepare student teachers for every topic they might teach, and teacher education programs count on cooperating teachers to fill many of these gaps. Student teachers need classroom experiences in how to use the various types of laboratory and demonstration equipment in their classroom and around the science department. Student teachers may never have operated gas sensor probes or van de Graaff generators before, and even if they are familiar with this equipment, learning to use these items pedagogically can often be challenging. Having the opportunity to practice and explore the use of science teaching equipment and other instructional technology with the guidance of a knowledgeable mentor is always a valuable use of time in the student teaching experience.

#6. Model How to Learn New Content as a Teacher.

Student teachers quickly learn that their content knowledge, strong as it is in certain areas, may not be nearly as deep or flexible as they might wish it to be. This can be frustrating and embarrassing and may make them feel inadequate and underprepared. Even the strongest among them will still be learning the science content, and it will likely show through in their teaching when fragments of their knowledge appear untethered to big ideas of the discipline.

Cooperating teachers who are honest with student teachers about their own learning, and exhibit a "growth mindset" are able to lay the groundwork for future conversations about understanding the content.[8] One approach is the use of rehearsals during preparations for lessons, in which a cooperating teacher may ask a student teacher to describe how they might explain a particular science idea to the students. If the student teacher has trouble with a lesson because of the content, a good mentor will not hesitate to give a mini-lesson on the spot to help clear things up.[9]

#7. Plan Together.

Having recently taken college courses that explore the upper reaches of their disciplines—like physical chemistry and molecular ecology—student teachers may forget what it is like to *not* know something simple, like Newton's laws, the periodic table, or basic cell structure. This is complicated because people who choose to become high school science teachers were likely high achievers as students themselves. Consequently, they may feel that they are dumbing down the curriculum when writing lessons and unit plans and worry that they are being unfaithful to their science disciplines when they modify lessons for different learners.

Planning together and continually asking, "What do we want the students to learn from this?" is important for these reasons. Student teachers benefit from both guidance on setting appropriate learning goals for students, and ongoing discussions about what constitutes acceptable evidence of meeting those goals. When framed this way, the intellectual challenge of planning may even appeal to the scientific problem-solving dispositions of student teachers.

#8. Make Time to Talk.

Even though student teachers and cooperating teachers work together daily, there may not be adequate time during the bustle of the school day to talk in-depth about how things are going. If there are important issues that need addressing, they will likely not get resolved on their own without conversation. Occasionally these are about matters outside of the classroom. Issues of professionalism, like timeliness or appropriate attire, are often of concern to cooperating teachers, while student teachers may be more preoccupied with the challenging nature of the experience of student teaching and its impact on their personal lives. Classroom management troubles often take precedence for student teachers, and a cooperating teacher's approach to talking through these issues will determine whether they will able to move beyond a fixation on student control to a focus on student learning. The cooperating teacher and student teacher ought to be able to express their expectations and needs at the beginning of the student teaching experience and subsequently keep their lines of communication open.

#9. Connect Student Teachers to the Larger Political World of the School.

Student teachers may express an interest in learning more about their legal rights and responsibilities as teachers. These may include questions about safety in the science classroom, school budgets, and how contract negotiations work, among other things. Learning about all of this is important, especially given how deeply politics—the processes by which people and power are organized in a society—influences the work of teaching, both in the classroom and in teachers' personal and professional lives. This helps them see the niche that a classroom teacher occupies in relation to the larger systems of the school and society as a whole.

Cooperating teachers can assist in providing student teachers opportunities to learn about and think through these issues in a number of ways. It is worthwhile for them to attend a school board meeting, meet community organizers, and talk to people who understand the history of the district and the school. Understanding the role of teachers' unions—which some places have, and others do not—and how the specific employment contract operates in a district is always beneficial. They can be shown what a teacher evaluation report looks like, and be encouraged to explore online documents like school testing data, state report cards, census data for the district, and the school budget.

As in every profession, novice teachers will hear stories about those who crossed ethical and legal lines (or were accused of doing so), some of whom encountered swift and severe consequences and others who faced none. The role of a mentoring figure is ensuring that novices consider the full complexity of these stories, and take away lessons from them that help foster—and not shut down—their professional growth.

Giving student teachers a sense of the different perspectives available on relevant issues at the level of the school and classroom is also very valuable. What are the discussions in the district around English language learners, gifted education, attendance areas, preparation periods, teacher duties, parent meetings, and the budget? What happens at meetings of child study teams? How are students selected for advanced science courses? What are the legal requirements for storing chemicals and keeping students safe in a lab? Student teachers who explore the answers to such inquiries will soon begin generating more and better questions—an outcome any good scientist can appreciate.

#10. Treat Student Teaching as a Learning Opportunity, Not as a Performance.

Many student teachers, as much as they would like to think otherwise, view their teaching as a performance, evaluating each lesson as a test that they either pass or fail. They often need help in reframing their work more clinically, with the view that there is something to be learned from each lesson. This may not be a student teacher's initial orientation, yet with sustained effort a mentor can cultivate such a disposition over time.

One way to do this is to have a candid talk prior to any observation about the use of evaluative language. There is nothing more natural than saying, "That lesson went well," to a student teacher after an observation, but such language can be counterproductive in the longer-term goals of improving practice and student learning because it feeds the impression that each lesson is to be judged. It is more productive to begin instead with the assumption that in each lesson there will be parts that are good and other parts that can be improved.

★★★

Mentoring a student teacher is both challenging and rewarding. The hard work that goes into helping someone learn how to teach is balanced by the benefit of having an enthusiastic apprentice, and taking advantage of this situation is essential for cooperating teachers' own professional learning. Cooperating teachers may even present student teachers with their own problems of practice to see what solutions they can offer. If there is a lab activity that needs improvement, or a bothersome classroom issue that persists over time, the student teacher may have unexpected insights. After all, they are often searching for new strategies themselves and may have an answer right at their fingertips. Being able to make the mentoring relationship mutually beneficial is one final lesson to student teachers about the value of humility and grace in life-long learning, which they will likely take with them as they grow over the years into mentors themselves.

Notes

1 The visit was a part of a project investigating the ways in which teachers engaged in reasoning about pedagogy and race, and was published as Larkin (2010, 2013). I am always grateful to teachers who open their classrooms to researchers like me.

2 Britzman (2003) suggests that the ideas and life experiences of teachers—the fundamental fabric of individual identity—also represent the raw material for crafting one's practice as a teacher. And just as identity influences conceptions about teaching, the reverse is also true. Learning to teach has the potential to affect one's beliefs, knowledge, and goals because of the way the experience of learning to teach compels the reinterpretation of past experience. This process cannot help but reshape one's conception of one's self and overall identity.

3 Hammerness et al., 2005.

4 Windschitl, 2003.

5 Larkin, 2012.

6 Abell, 2007.

7 Zeichner & Conklin, 2005; Zeichner & Gore, 1990.

8 The research on growth vs. performance orientations pioneered by Carol Dweck (2006) has deep implications for teaching and learning. Briefly, individuals with a *performance* orientation place a higher value on the evaluation of a performance (such as in an athletic competition, stage performance, or in the case of teaching, a lesson), while individuals with a *growth* orientation seek feedback so that they can improve future performances.

9 Educator Eleanor Duckworth notes that lectures have the greatest efficacy when the learner already holds a basic understanding of most of the material (Harvard-Smithsonian Center for Astrophysics & Annenberg/CPB Project, 2000), which is likely the case for many pre-service teachers in their student teaching placements. What a good lecture does is to help the learner organize information in a new and more flexible way in order to facilitate future retrieval (Bransford et al., 1999).

13

THE BLACK BELT SCIENCE TEACHER

Differentiation and a Speculative Learning Progression for Science Teachers

Both children in our family have been involved in karate, and I have spent countless hours watching them learn new skills and practice ones they have already learned. From the sidelines, I found myself thinking increasingly about the colored belts that separate the different skill levels in many martial arts, and what that particular system of performance assessment might be able to teach those of us concerned with the professional growth of teachers.

When a karate student begins instruction and has made the commitment to continue learning—initially by simply continuing to show up—they are issued a white belt. Over time, as students acquire skills, techniques, and routines and then demonstrate mastery of them to instructors and recognized experts, they earn the belt of the next rank. Though many martial arts use colored belts for ranking, within each tradition there are very specific indicators of what separates one level of performance from another. There is also a clear expectation that practices learned in earlier belts continue to be worked on and refined. Routines and skills that once seemed to stand alone as distinctive practices are revealed over time to have been components of more complex actions, and prior mastery of the earlier moves has a tangible payoff.

Could a similar system be applied to teaching? I approach such a project cautiously, recognizing that the history of teacher education is littered with exhaustive attempts to outline the knowledge and skills that teachers need, and that many of these approaches have borne limited fruit; after all, there has not always been a broad consensus about the purposes of education, let alone agreement upon what constitutes good teaching. Still, I cannot help but ponder the vision of black belt science teaching, and I am stirred by the idea that those of us involved in teacher education and teacher development could make such a system a reality.

Such a thing has happened before, when the National Board Certification was dreamed into existence in the 1980s.[1]

★★★

When I think about the hundreds of science classrooms that I have visited over my twenty-five years as an educator, I suspect that I have seen black belt science teaching only a handful of times. One particular classroom that comes to mind is that of Mr. H., a middle school physical science teacher in a prairie community in Wisconsin. The first time I visited him was simply to confirm a student teacher placement, and when I entered there were eight different groups of students all doing slightly different inquiry labs with the same apparatus setup. Mr. H. stood in the center of the room like an air traffic controller, aware of everything that was going on but keeping the communication to a minimum, letting the students pilot themselves as much as possible. He explained to me that the differentiated lab structure he was using was the product of a long career, shaped by intentional reflective practice around goals he set for himself as an educator. In the few minutes we talked, he fielded minor procedural questions from students, caught a few safety concerns, and multi-tasked like a professional, but I noticed that he did not seem overly stressed out, the way my student teachers typically are during a lab, and most of the students seemed to be operating autonomously and deeply involved their work, in sharp contrast to most classrooms I visit. His students were doing science because he had created the classroom conditions to make that possible.

Mr. H. involved prospective teachers in such a way that at once treated them as an equal while offering them an opportunity to learn from his wisdom of practice. He also quite clearly expected to learn from them, thus modeling the role of a lifelong learner that we expected our program graduates to adopt. I wished I could put every one of my student teachers in Mr. H.'s classroom to learn from him. He let me stay to watch the class for a while, and it was glorious.

★★★

The practice of differentiated instruction, which made such an impression on me in Mr. H.'s classroom, will serve here to illustrate the idea of applying something like karate belt levels to teacher learning. I choose this particular practice because it is very difficult for novice teachers to do well, even when they are strongly motivated to try. In my professional judgment, a well-differentiated classroom is a mark of a master teacher. On more than one occasion, I have heard administrators and supervisors urge novice teachers to engage in advanced differentiation practices. While well intentioned, this seems like expecting someone who just learned a few karate moves to chop through a stack of cinder blocks.

Differentiation is a tricky concept, and operates as one of those education buzzwords that has different meanings in different contexts. Historically, differentiation was related to the sorting function of schooling, and was synonymous to what we now call "tracking".[2] There is also differentiation of the one-roomed schoolhouse variety, such as those that exist in island schools off the coast of Maine, where a single teacher is responsible for teaching a wide age-range of students. Here, I refer to differentiation as the provision of multiple pathways in a classroom towards a learning goal within a particular age-level or subject area.

Educator James Delisle (2015) began a vigorous debate a few years back in the pages of Education Week with a critique of differentiation as unrealistic for most teachers. "Although fine in theory," he said, "differentiation in practice is harder to implement in a heterogeneous classroom than it is to juggle with one arm tied behind your back," (p. 28). For a white-belt teacher, that is likely true. But such a trick is certainly possible for teachers at the black-belt level who have engaged in patient study, systematic reflection, and sustained practice of differentiation skills over time. The error is thinking that teachers can learn how to do it quickly and with minimal effort.

In this theoretical belt system, teachers would begin with a clear goal of what knowledge and skills needed to be acquired and mastered. They would be able to access models of what exemplary practices look like through videos, real-time observation of peers, or even computer simulations.[3] Detailed feedback on their efforts to enact such practices in the classroom would be provided to them by knowledgeable experts, and teachers would elect to demonstrate their mastery to a panel of evaluators when they felt prepared to do so. Success would advance them toward new knowledge, skills, and practices at the next level.

For novice teachers (at a white belt level, here), practices of differentiated instruction would be primarily focused on compliance with school, district, and state policies. Teachers of students with individualized educational plans (IEPs), as well as teachers of students with limited English proficiency, are obligated to ensure that all students have the opportunity to learn, and that all legal requirements are met. There is also ample reason from the research to believe that novice teachers are able engage in practices that permit every student in the class to access the curriculum through equitable teaching.[4] In the richest descriptions of differentiated instruction (representing black belt teaching here), students are in charge of their own learning, know what they need to accomplish to demonstrate their attainment of the next objective in a learning progression, and may be working individually or collaboratively on worthwhile tasks. In these classrooms, it may look as if the teacher is not doing much at all beyond rudimentary scaffolding for the class and serving as a resource to students in their own learning.[5]

★★★

As an intellectual exercise, I here sketch out one possible progression of what a belt system might look like, at least in regard to differentiated instruction, as teachers master each level of proficiency. One lesson from the last three decades of teacher assessment research is that subject matter and student developmental level play an important role, even as there are practices that cut across all grades and disciplines. Here then is what it might look like for a secondary science teacher to advance through a series of such belt-levels. For the purposes of this example I will move through the belt levels in what is to me a convenient order: white, yellow, orange, green, blue, red, and black, because it generally corresponds to the sequence I observed my own children following in their karate classes.

For a novice teacher who has successfully completed a teacher preparation program, and is state-certified to teach science at the early adolescent level, the awarding of the teaching certificate may be considered to be equivalent to receiving a white belt. This signals the accomplishment of being admitted to the profession while communicating that the real learning is just beginning.[6]

White Belt Testing for Yellow belt: Ensuring Curricular Access and Engaging in Equity Pedagogy

> *Performance expectation:* design and implement a lesson in which students will engage in scientific inquiry. Craft the instructions of the activity in a way that ensures curricular access for all students, including students from diverse backgrounds, students who are English language learners, and students with individual education plans.

At this belt level, science teachers would demonstrate not only that they can meet their legal obligations as teachers, but also that they are able to modify their instruction in order to ensure that all students in the class have an opportunity to achieve. Note that nothing in the performance expectation requires a teacher to work alone. Indeed, it would be quite appropriate for a teacher to work with a special education teacher or assistant in order to modify handouts and assessments, or make the necessary physical and technological accommodations so that students could fully participate in the lesson.

Yellow Belt Testing for Orange Belt: Working with Student Ideas/ Multiple Paths

> *Performance expectation:* demonstrate a phenomenon to students that is specifically connected or otherwise representative of a big idea in science. Elicit students' ideas about this phenomenon, and design a lesson that uses those ideas in a meaningful way. The lesson should allow students to examine, refine, and revise their ideas, and permit them to follow different learning pathways in order to make sense of the content in light of the big science idea.

Viewed from the perspective of other arguments about science teaching made earlier in this book, this performance expectation seems rather tame, primarily because it reflects the modern consensus within the science education community, prominent in recent standards documents. What makes it challenging as a performance, however, is the expectation that it be carried out in a way that is consistent with—instead of separate from—the previous expectation for curricular access and equity pedagogy.

Differentiated instruction is slightly concealed here, but the act of eliciting student ideas and designing instruction that takes them into account is an integral component of every subsequent task, and thus ought to be mastered early on. Doing so also reinforces the importance of leveraging the linguistic and cultural resources of students, in addition to the knowledge and ideas they bring with them from their life experiences. Differentiating instruction is predicated on having a relatively complete understanding of the learners in a class, and the practice of eliciting students' ideas helps to put that picture together.

Orange Belt Testing for Green Belt: Designing Assessments Tasks at Different Levels of Challenge

Performance expectation: prepare a set of assessment tasks for a lesson at three levels of challenge, designed to give students feedback about their progress toward class learning goals. Help students choose the task at the appropriate level of challenge and make any necessary adjustments to the tasks during the lesson based on student performance. It is important that the corresponding assessment of students' work provide information about students' understanding of the science content, regardless of the learning pathway the student follows.

It is at this belt level that the ideas of differentiated instruction as advocated by researchers and teacher evaluation systems begin coming into focus. Rather than use labels for assessment tasks that run the risk of also applying to students (e.g. basic, average, advanced), thoughtful advocates of differentiated instruction suggest describing the nature of the tasks themselves, such as with labels like "straight ahead," "uphill," and "mountainous."[7]

Sometimes teachers who attempt to differentiate their classrooms get stuck on the feedback part, and I have seen well-intentioned science teachers create a grading backlog for themselves that is nearly impossible to escape. Being able to provide detailed and useful feedback in a timely and efficient manner is not something that can easily be done without careful forethought and planning, and clearly having more time and resources also makes a difference. It is also the case that students who previously operated autonomously might suddenly need a whole lot more help if they are being challenged in ways they previously had not. Figuring out how to provide feedback that responds to students' efforts at sense-making from various learning pathways is the central challenge of this belt level.[8]

Green Belt Testing for Blue Belt: Grouping and Collaboration

Performance expectation: design and implement a lesson that uses a grouping of students based on readiness, interest, or students' learning profiles, and provide the opportunity for students to learn discipline-specific scientific practices that will be necessary to complete the task(s) in the lesson. It is important that groups are able to choose an appropriate level of challenge, and collaborate effectively and equitably.

The ability to use flexible grouping strategies is a hallmark of differentiated instruction. On its own, it is a strategy commonly employed in thousands of classrooms on a daily basis, but is much more difficult to achieve when enacted with the three practices described previously.

Novice teachers often assess the quality of group collaboration through inelegant prompts that force students to rate each other, which can cause unnecessary anxiety or conflict among group members. In contrast, master teachers have figured out how to assess student collaboration in ways that respect the need for students to retain their dignity, yet still provide necessary feedback to improve the group's performance. This is no easy feat, and requires a depth of understandings about both psychology and the use of language.

Blue Belt Testing for Red Belt: Fine-grained Assessment

> *Performance expectation:* design a way to assess student learning of the big ideas and scientific practices in such a way that students are able to obtain a clear understanding of their individual progress toward learning goals, allowing for a variety of work products accepted as evidence. Develop a system for keeping track of individual students' progress towards specific learning goals, and practices, and systematize this so that every student in the class understands where they are and what comes next.

Individualized instruction and assessment is enjoying a certain amount of popularity in the current educational climate, particularly as a consequence of technological advances like computer-based adaptive testing and learning management systems. Like flexible grouping however, implementing an individualized instruction and assessment system is much easier when attempted as a stand-alone project or with a single student, and much more challenging when it is integrated with a whole class into an existing series of practices like the earlier belt levels described here. Certainly, it is likely that technology can play a role in a teacher's ability to provide detailed individual feedback to students about where they are and where they need to go next, but it may not be absolutely necessary.

As part of this effort, science teachers can learn a great deal from early childhood literacy teachers, because of the common practice of keeping detailed records about where students are in their ability to read, and then using this information to suggest books at the next appropriate level of difficulty. Similarly, a chemistry teacher could choose to keep detailed records on a few key indicators, such as students' ability to read markings on graduated glassware correctly, make connections between atomic structure and the periodic table, or solve stoichiometry problems of varying difficulty. Though demonstrating mastery of fine-grained assessment might be limited to a specific moment in time, it is likely that in order to earn this belt, it would need to be systematized seamlessly into everyday classroom teaching.

Red Belt Testing for Black Belt: Scheduling and Self-regulation

> *Performance expectation:* prepare a lesson in which students are using time flexibly across multiple class periods or days. Demonstrate that students can schedule their own learning plan (which may include teacher-directed or whole-class components), self-regulate their intellectual engagement, and self-assess their progress toward specific learning goals.

At first glance, this expectation appears to be more appropriate to doctoral study than a middle or high school science classroom, but in many ways this depiction of teaching and learning reflects the outcomes recommended throughout a range of panel reports, teacher evaluation systems, and standards documents, all of which highlight the role of self-assessment and metacognition in learning.[9]

There is no reason that a teacher needs to wait until this level to attempt to use classroom strategies in which students self-assess or make their own learning plans. However, this is logistically the most challenging of all of the performance expectations discussed here because all of the other learning experiences, tasks, assessments, and grouping components need to be in place to make it work.

Recognizing that I risk stretching my metaphor to its breaking point, it is instructive to consider what lies beyond the black belt.[10] In martial arts, when a student has earned a black belt, it is appropriate to become a mentor, a leader, and even a teacher. I envision black-belt science teachers looking for ways to improve science teaching and learning across their schools, and working with novice teachers to assist them in their own journeys toward mastery. In terms of differentiated instruction, this could entail advocacy for equity-based differentiation practices across grades, subject disciplines, or throughout the entire school.

★★★

One critique that could be fairly leveled at this whole system of teacher learning is that so much of a teacher's ability to enact these practices in a given classroom depends tremendously on the students. It is not difficult to imagine a set of students in one school context being far more accommodating to a teacher's efforts to differentiate instruction than students in a different school. I do not disagree that these tasks are very student-dependent, and it seems entirely plausible that it might take a teacher seven years in one school to become a black belt science teacher, while in another school it might take fifteen years.[11]

However, one of the practices of the white belt teachers—something that every beginning teacher ought to know and be able to do—is to study their students, both individually and as members of the school community. This is a necessary precondition for being able to choose relevant phenomena and elicitation strategies, as well as to understand the varied forms of communication that students use to demonstrate their learning to us as teachers.

Bruce Lee, the influential martial artist and actor, wrote about his own pedagogy of karate, which was an integral part of his rise to fame. From the vantage point of the present day, this seems remarkably prescient and applicable to the growth of teachers:

> A teacher, a really good sensei, is never a *giver* of "truth"; he is a guide, a *pointer* to the truth that the student must discover for himself. A good teacher, therefore, studies each student individually and encourages the student to explore himself, both internally and externally, until, ultimately, the student is integrated with his being...A good teacher is a catalyst. Besides possessing deep understanding, he must also have a responsive mind with great flexibility and sensitivity.[12]

★★★

The learning progression I have outlined here is the equivalent of an engineering prototype or proof-of-concept. It does not yet exist in the real world of teacher learning, but the components that could build this system are out there in schools right now. When I think about what science teaching might look like a century or two from now, it is comforting to envision every child learning from a black belt master.

Notes

1 In the introduction to *What Teachers Should Know and Be Able to Do* (National Board of Professional Teaching Standards, 2016), Lee Shulman describes the early dreams of what National Board Certification might look like. "We set out to imagine a new institution, owned and operated by America's most accomplished teachers, designing standards and inventing forms of assessment that had never existed before. When we began to dream that dream and discussed it with colleagues, our visions were initially dismissed as hallucinations, as fantasies without a needed grounding in reality," (p. 3). Thirty years later, the National Board of Professional Teaching Standards has certified over 112,000 teachers through a rigorous and innovative portfolio-based process.
2 See Oakes (2005).
3 The World Language Teaching Video Library described by Zhai (2019) is one discipline-specific example. Classroom simulations like the TeachLive program developed by the University of Central Florida (e.g. Speed, Bradley, & Garland, 2015), combined with immersive virtual reality technology likely mean that we will have a working "holodeck" for teachers someday in the near future as imagined by Fenstermacher and Richardson's (2005) thought experiment about teacher quality. An associated challenge for critical educators is to ensure that current and future technology do not serve to encode and reinscribe systemic biases and inequalities into these new systems (O'Neil, 2016; Wachter-Boettcher, 2017).
4 Goodlad, Mantle-Bromley, & Goodlad, 2004; Hammerness et al., 2005; Meyer et al., 2016
5 One prominent proponent of differentiated instruction is Carol Ann Tomlinson (1999), who argues that differentiation is a basic tenet of instruction. Without a commitment to equity however, differentiated instruction can easily lead to academic tracking, which is widely considered problematic despite its continued use in many schools (National Research Council, 2002; Oakes, 2005). In teacher evaluation instruments such as the Framework for Teaching (Danielson, 2007), principles of

differentiated instruction are evident in the "Distinguished" level of performance indicators. For a brief description and history of the modern concept of differentiated instruction, see Sparks (2015).

6 My friend Gordon Perkins, a longtime science teacher at Memorial High School in Madison, Wisconsin, tells a story about taking flying lessons and eventually earning his pilot's license. When his instructor signed the official document and handed it to him, he said, "This is your ticket to keep learning."

7 Tomlinson and McTighe, 2006.

8 One approach to solving the problem of formative assessment in the differentiated classroom is through the use of standards-based grading (Wormeli, 2018).

9 These include the National Academy of Sciences reports *How People Learn* (Bransford et al., 1999), *Taking Science to School*, (National Research Council, 2007), and the *Next Generation Science Standards* (Achieve Inc., 2013).

10 In many martial arts, the levels of black belts continue to second-degree, third-degree, etc.

11 Consequently, such a system would not be good for teacher evaluation or for implementing policies like merit pay.

12 Lee, 1971.

14

TEACHING AT THE BOUNDARIES OF OUR KNOWLEDGE

Being Knowledgeable Enough About What We Teach to Not Feel Like a Fraud

Here are a few real-life scenarios that have nightmare potential for some science teachers: a first-grade teacher who has used the *Rock, Sand, & Soil* kit each fall for a decade, and has integrated it throughout her literacy instruction, suddenly finds out two weeks before the start of the school year that the kits are unavailable and that she will need to teach a unit on motion instead. A middle school life science teacher is told that because of declining school enrollment, he is being shuffled from 7th grade to 8th grade, where he will be expected to teach units on astronomy, oceanography, weather, and plate tectonics that he has not taught before. A physics teacher shows up to the faculty meeting the day before school starts and is surprised to be handed a schedule that includes one earth science class, which technically he is certified to teach, but has never done so. In each of these cases, teachers are put in situations where they may be forced to stay just a few steps ahead of their students. They must teach at the boundaries of their own knowledge. For some teachers this is invigorating, while others worry that stepping off the path of certainty carries the risk of being revealed as a fraud.

Ideally, teachers ought to be eased into such transitions, and be provided with ample time and support to learn or refamiliarize themselves with the content prior to teaching it. Such teachers would also need to acquaint themselves with the curriculum, the various ways to make the subject understandable to students, and the ideas that students are likely to hold. But it is also true that sometimes even within a given subject area, there are topics beyond the comfortable and familiar that can even seem a bit intimidating.

As a teacher educator, I have seen this with biology student teachers who may feel quite at home in environmental science but are daunted by topics in molecular biology (or vice versa). Similarly, physics students who have been doing differential equations in their thermodynamics upper elective courses, might experience a crisis of confidence when asked to prepare a lesson on linear motion. The irony is that the complex parts of content may seem easy to communicate—especially if the equations, specialized notation, and advanced vocabulary teachers encountered in college are used—yet figuring out how to convey basic ideas to students can be maddeningly difficult.

Science teachers know that designing instruction on topics we may initially know little about is a perfectly normal part of our job, and even if it takes effort, many do actually enjoy learning science that is new to them. The hard part is that this content has to be learned in a way that allows for it to be teachable. Even with significant time and effort dedicated to the task of mastering new science content, it is easy to feel like a fraud in front of students when we are not completely sure about what we are teaching. One teacher I observed had received perfect grades in his undergraduate biology classes, and was therefore surprised and more than a little frustrated as he struggled to teach an immunology unit in a high school biology class. He said that he was "just keeping ahead of the students," and often felt like he was not doing his job if he was not able to answer students' questions.[1]

★★★

One of the reasons that unfamiliar topics can seem overwhelming to many science teachers is that there just seems to be so much to know. Teachers with an apprehension about teaching a particular science topic may feel an ethical responsibility not to inflict their own attitudes and confusion about science on their own students—a mark of thoughtful teachers who want to do a good job.

Different teachers respond in different ways to a need to learn new science content. Some lean almost entirely on their curriculum materials, and are more than happy to outsource curricular thinking about the unit to a teachers' guide.[2] Other teachers learn enough of the content so as not to feel foolish in front of their students, but recognize they lack adequate time to develop expertise. Then there are the teachers who throw themselves into learning the subject matter, trusting that their patient study will be rewarded with understanding. Many teachers find knowledgeable colleagues who they feel comfortable asking for support, who can talk through and help unlock the big ideas in the topic. Those with a measure of humility may even acknowledge their own knowledge gaps in front of their students, and are willing to answer difficult student questions with, "I don't know, let's find out."

A college degree in a science field is easy to interpret as a consumer guarantee that someone knows his or her subject well enough to teach it to children, and most parents and administrators generally hope that this is true. Having a biology teacher who does not completely understand immunology, or a chemistry teacher who cannot describe Le Chatelier's Principle, is seen as somehow equivalent to selling a defective product. Even elementary teachers, who are expected to have expertise across multiple subject areas, may be criticized for not knowing basic science concepts, despite decades of research that show how difficult some things—like Newton's first law of motion—are to learn. Teachers, of course, do not wish to be perceived as ignorant, and so there is a natural tendency to start accumulating bits of trivia about a topic as a way to project a certain level of confidence. The problem with this approach is that the manner in which knowledge within a given subject or topic is organized tends to be rather important to mastering it. This can create the tension that may make a teacher—especially a novice—feel like a fraud.

***

At the risk of oversimplifying, there are two broad categories of missing content knowledge for science teachers. The first is the big stuff—whole swaths of subject matter with which a teacher has little passing familiarity. State accountability measures may refer to this as "teaching out of certification," like when a biology teacher has to teach physics. It can also be something that a teacher is technically licensed to teach, but simply has not previously taught.

Then there are the smaller things, the anomalies, which are much more socially acceptable for teachers not to know because they seem so minor. I contend that attending to these little mysteries also has value. Anomalies in our own understanding are often portals to "aha" moments that help us make connections we did not see originally, and exploring our way through them can lead to new insights. Another reason I like these little investigations is because they make us act upon the knowledge we have, which some argue is a much better criteria for actually claiming to know things because the knowledge is not separate from its use.[3]

***

So here are some tangible suggestions for teachers who set out to learn some new science:

Remember what it is like not to know. When embarking on learning a new topic in order to eventually teach it, there is value at pausing at the outset to take note of what it feels like not to know. This may come in handy later if it leads to new insights on how to present the topic to students in a similar situation.[4]

Take stock of your own prior knowledge. Personally, I find it tempting to overestimate the importance of what I already know. Some deeply-lodged fact in my brain may have come from an overheard remark from thirty years ago, and the only reason I attach importance to it is because I have remembered it for so long. Such facts may not even be true, yet are part of what we bring to the act of learning.

Get a sense for how the field is organized. Any attempt to simply acquire a surplus of facts about a topic is likely to result in extreme frustration and despair. It is far better to begin by getting a sense for how the subject matter is organized around its big ideas. Standards documents can be extraordinarily helpful because they are arranged in precisely this way, while textbooks can be misleading because they are organized by topic. Drawing concept maps can be a helpful way to figure out how the topic is structured.

Figure out how we know what we know. Phenomena exist independently of humans, but knowledge itself does not. When we ask where knowledge comes from, what we are really doing is seeking justification and backing for knowledge claims. As a novice physics teacher who had to cover a biology class for two months, I found the task of memorizing organelles and their functions set for students in the lesson plans I was left to be particularly tedious. Digging into the evidence for mitochondria existing in deep time as a separate organism, however, was quite satisfying. The reward was more than just a better understanding of the content, because making sense of the arguments and evidence for endosymbiotic theory gave me an insight into the operation of certain scientific practices in molecular biology, which were quite different from what I was familiar with in physics.

Find connections to other big science ideas. To me this is the most exciting aspect of learning new science, because insights driven by making connections to other science ideas—particularly the ones we already know well—tend to make a lasting impression. As a new teacher, the connections between dinosaur bones and nuclear half-life only became clear to me as I struggled to understand how scientists could determine the age of a fossil.[5] While seemingly familiar at the outset, actually making sense of radiometric dating as a scientific tool was something wholly different, and opened up a new world of understanding for me.

Look for ways the topic connects to people, and especially students. Keeping an eye open for connections to human activity and puzzling phenomena helps teachers to answer the "so what?" question for their students. If we as teachers cannot give good reasons for knowing why people should care about whether rocks are sedimentary, igneous, or metamorphic, neither will the students.[6]

As a Peace Corps volunteer in East Africa, I once witnessed a marvelous moment with a Kenyan science teacher that illustrates this point. Mr. Makhoha and I were chaperoning our school's sports teams at an away game, and were standing on top of a very large expanse of rock on the sidelines in a gentle rain. As we waited with our girls for their turn on the field, he directed their attention to a puddle of water on top of the rock, gathering them around it. "Think about the properties of this rock," he told them. "Would you want to build a water tank out of this kind of rock?" It was a teachable moment in which he took the students' answers and applied labels like *permeable* and *impermeable* to the ideas they shared. He was teaching them—in a culturally relevant manner to be sure, because the availability of clean water was an everyday socioeconomic issue in their lives—why they should care about different types of rock. As we chart our own learning path into science, it is worthwhile to stay mindful of potential opportunities to make these kinds of connections with our own students.

Keep a running list of things to learn. Ever since becoming a teacher, I have kept a running list of things I do not know, and nothing feels better than figuring out a mystery that has simmered in that kettle for a long time.[7] As teachers, we know that one of the fundamentally important principles of learning is being metacognitive—thinking about thinking—and doing this for ourselves as we engage in our own scientific sensemaking pays off handsomely. There are times when it is also necessary to dive back into mathematics in order to know something well enough to teach it—I am thinking of the first time I taught pH in a chemistry class and had to finally reckon with logarithms. Being honest with oneself about areas of struggle is a good first step to actually learning.

Look for the edges of the science itself. When the opportunity arises to talk to scientists about what they do, I always like to ask what the big unresolved questions are in their field. The answers say a lot about the edges, not just of our own knowledge, but also of science itself. Biologists right now are trying to figure out how to predict the structure and properties of a protein from its amino acid sequence, which turns out to be surprisingly difficult.[8] Chemists continue to be surprised by the strange properties of materials at the nanoscale, and physicists have the vexing mystery of dark matter and dark energy. Then there are all of the other open areas of inquiry that are much more applied and pragmatic, like how to store energy from renewable sources, model climate change, and safely clean up hazardous waste in rivers.

★★★

In many ways, it is easier to remain unfamiliar with a large section of scientific knowledge than it is to ignore something that one feels ought to be already known. Like most small but persistent problems, a missing piece of knowledge is often better addressed directly rather neglected. Avoiding problematic content can easily lead to building detours around it or even dismissing it as unimportant, and this can negatively impact teachers and students alike. A phrase I learned in Kenya was that it was better to remove the pebble from one's shoe rather than learn how to limp. I wish to end this chapter with a brief story of removing one such pebble from my intellectual shoe, only to learn that I had been limping along the whole time.

In my first year of teaching high school chemistry, a minor detail about the periodic table bothered me a great deal. It had to do with all the decimal places in measurements of atomic mass. As a high school student, I was perfectly content with the idea of average atomic mass—that the number on the periodic table listing an element's atomic mass was an average of the slightly different masses of an element's isotopes proportional to abundance. Measured in atomic mass units, carbon's periodic table square lists its average atomic mass at 12.011, and the explanation that the extra 11 thousandths came from a tiny bit of heavier carbon-14 mixed in with the carbon-12, made sense. Somewhere in my science learning history I had done a lab with old and new pennies that made this perfectly clear to me.[9]

But the thing that made me nervous was that I was unable to explain why the numbers were not clean integers when just dealing with a single isotope. I accepted the idea that neutrons could be responsible, yet why was the mass of carbon-12 with six protons and neutrons (12 atomic mass units) less than the mass of six protons and six neutrons individually?[10] If I weigh six apples and six oranges together, they will weigh exactly the same as the sum of their individual weights. Not so with protons and neutrons. The missing mass was about 0.5% of the mass of a carbon atom. My students were accustomed to not worrying too much about decimal places when it came to taking measurements, and the numbers were so small that I initially did not feel too bad waving the difference away. However, I genuinely worried that if any student ever asked me about this, I would instantly be revealed as a fraud because I knew that those decimals were not just random digits on a periodic table. There were reasons for them being there that I did not understand. I asked the other chemistry teachers in my department, and nobody had any answers.[11]

I was perfectly comfortable saying, "I don't know, let's find out" to my students when confronted by run-of-the-mill questions like: could a penny dropped from the top of a skyscraper actually kill a person?[12] However, there was something about this atomic mass question that greatly bothered me because it genuinely seemed like something a chemistry teacher ought to know.[13] As I wrestled with the day-to-day demands of being a first-year teacher with six classes in three subjects in four different rooms, the question about the missing atomic mass continued to gnaw at me.

If I were a new teacher now, I could probably just look up the answer on the Internet, but that was not an option in 1993, at least in my town. Instead, I decided one day to spend my lunch period in the library, and found my answer in an old chemistry book.

Growing up, I was as familiar with Albert Einstein as everyone else, and the formula $E=mc^2$ was shorthand for all things scientific. It was probably the first algebraic formula I ever learned. Which is why I was so shocked when I discovered that it held the answer to my question. The energy that had been released when all of those protons and neutrons had come together in the first place came from the mass of the individual particles. That missing mass in the carbon atom had been *converted* into energy—which could be described by the relationship between mass and energy in the formula $E=mc^2$. So not only did I feel like I could explain the chemistry answer of the missing mass, for the first time I felt like I had a conceptual understanding that helped explain some of my physics as well. There was much more to learn—such as why fusion occurred only in atoms with atomic numbers lower than that of iron—and the fact that I remember this moment 25 years later likely says something about its importance to me as a learner.

★★★

One thing that I make sure to do with every student teacher I work with is to give them explicit permission not to be perfect. University teacher education programs are generally quite clear about who they expect their teachers to be as professionals, and the programs in which I have worked are no different. Having a vision of what good science teaching looks like is important to prospective and current science teachers alike, and this vision includes the teacher as a subject matter expert who can provide access to knowledge for all students. Yet, a vision of good science teaching is by its very nature aspirational, and there will be days when any teacher falls short. There will be times when promising strategies in class fail spectacularly. There will be days when a sad morning phone call casts a pall over the whole day's lessons, and weeks when the teachers' guide must be leaned upon heavily. And there will be moments in full view of the students—sometimes in front of a board of physics equations—when everything suddenly seems wrong. Teachers are fallible human beings like everyone else, and the only time we are a truly fraud to our students is when we fail to acknowledge this fact.

Notes

1 This of course, reveals a particular conception of teaching science, in which the role of the teacher is to answer students' questions. Other science teachers may see their role as creating a learning environment in which students can answer their own questions.

2 More than once, I have encountered middle school teachers who sequence their kit-based units in such a way so that the unit they like the least falls at the end of the year, intentionally short-changing the amount of time allotted to it.

3 This is the argument put forth for the concept of situated cognition by Brown, Collins, and Duguid (1989): "Recent investigations of learning…challenge this separating of what is learned from how it is learned and used. The activity in which knowledge is developed and deployed, it is now argued, is not separable from or ancillary to learning and cognition. Nor is it neutral. Rather, it is an integral part of what is learned. Situations might be said to co-produce knowledge through activity. Learning and cognition, it is now possible to argue, are fundamentally situated." (p. 32) Perkins (1998) makes a similar argument about the nature of what it means to "understand" something.

4 Gee (2003) suggests that there is a great deal to learn about teaching and learning from playing video games. In particular, he suggests that when teachers play a difficult video game for the first time, they are able to experience what it feels like not to know how to do something, so as to empathize with the way students in their classrooms may feel when confronted with new and challenging topics.

5 "What does it mean to assign an age to a rock?" is a great essential question.

6 I rather like the idea that every rock tells a story, and that taken together, the stories of all the rocks on earth paint a powerful historical picture. Knowing rocks and the clues they offer (fossils, plate tectonics, radioactive dating, isotopic signatures) helps us tell the story of who we are as people on this planet.

7 At the top of my list for years now has been the question of why the law of reflection holds for light. A laser beam aimed at a mirror will reflect at an angle equal to the incoming angle. For a bouncing basketball on a floor, I can construct force diagrams that make sense of the equal angles, but for photons in a light beam interacting with atoms, I cannot come up with a reason for why all the photons all get emitted in the same direction by the mirror atoms that absorb them. I am aware that quantum electrodynamics is part of the answer, and that there is a Feymanesque sum-over-histories explanation as well, but I suspect there is a more satisfying way to make sense of this most elemental of optical laws. I have bothered many physics professors about this.

8 Even harder is understanding how a particular protein operates within the cellular ecology with all the other proteins and macromolecules. Decoding the human genome

set up the problem of the proteome. Beyond that is mapping the connectome of the neurons in the brain. Looks like it might be turtles all the way down.

9   Pre-1982 pennies were made of solid copper, and have a mass of 3.1 g, but after 1982 pennies were made of zinc and only coated with copper, and had a mass of only 2.5 g. Any mix of pennies is going to have an average mass between 2.5 and 3.1 depending on how many of each there are. Students can use algebra to figure out how many of each there are, giving their math teachers some relief to the question, "When are we ever going to use this?" If there are n pennies, and z is the number of old zinc pennies, then the total mass $m = 2.5z + 3.1(n-z)$. Plugging in the measurements for the total mass and the number of pennies, students can solve for the number of zinc pennies.

10   One atom of carbon 12 has a mass of 1.9927×10^{-23} g. The mass of six protons (6 x 1.6726×10^{-24} g) and six neutrons (6 x 1.6749×10^{-24} g) is: 2.0085×10^{-23} g.

11   In later years, I came to suspect that one teacher actually did know the answer, but she chose not to rob me of the pleasure of figuring all of this out for myself.

12   That one actually became an essential question that was useful for a few weeks in physics. Then, with perfect timing, this urban legend was actually tested on the show "Mythbusters" (Rees, 17 Oct 2003).

13   Really, one of the central problems was that I was not at all prepared as a chemistry teacher. I had exactly two chemistry courses in college, not counting the modern and quantum physics courses that approached chemistry from a very different direction. Even though I had earned a physical science certification from the state, which allowed me to teach physics and chemistry, my chemistry knowledge was quite flimsy. During my job interview, when the principal asked me if I thought I could teach chemistry, I thought back to an interview with a movie actor I had seen. She had been up for a big part, and at the end of the audition the director had asked if she knew how to ride a horse. "Of course!" she told the director, and immediately started learning how to ride a horse after she got the part. "Of course I can teach chemistry," I told the principal about to offer me the position, and then immediately started studying chemistry.

15

PLAYING SCHOOL VS. DOING SCIENCE

Providing All Students with Access to the Means of Knowledge Generation

In advertisements and stock photos, it is not uncommon to see glassware of different shapes and sizes filled with colored liquid used to convey an impression of scientific activity. When accompanied by people in white lab coats wearing safety goggles, the scene is a cultural signifier that communicates intelligence, curiosity, and persistence in pursuit of solutions to challenging problems. When selling expertise, this vision upholds a common stereotype of scientists as extraordinary people.

School science has similar signifiers of expertise and exclusivity. We have our safety goggles and lab coats too, along with Bunsen burners, test tube racks, graduated cylinders, black lab tables, Van de Graaff generators, dissection sets, microscopes, fruit fly vials with bright blue bottoms, eyewash stations, mineral samples, chemical storage rooms, acid and base cabinets, periodic table charts, wave tanks, aquariums, pH paper, drawers filled with two-holed rubber stoppers, three-dimensional tabletop models of flower parts, resin skeletons, air tracks, beakers, quad graph paper, photogates, dropper bottles of universal indicator, ticker tape timers, electromagnets, mercury switches, fume hoods, multimeters, fire blankets, ring stands, FOSS kits, boiling chips, fish tanks, clay triangles, filter paper, specimen jars in old wooden cabinets, Petri dishes, black and red wires with alligator clips, lenses of different sizes in small paper envelopes, diffraction gratings, squeeze bottles of bromothymol blue and methyl orange, fetal pigs wrapped in thick plastic, long-handled bottle brushes, boxes of prepared microscope slides arranged like venetian blinds, compasses on lanyards, force tables, tuning forks, black rubber aprons, triple-beam balances, and Teflon-coated magnets that, when dropped into an Erlenmeyer flask filled with colored water and placed on a laboratory stirring hotplate, generates a vortex that can convince the uninitiated that magic is real. It is all the more maddening that in so many classrooms, students can be surrounded by such trappings of scientific activity, yet still not engage in any real science.[1] In our most impoverished schools, the trappings are as absent as the science.

Throughout this book, I have presented the argument that a core intellectual task for science teachers is making subject matter accessible to their students.[2] In this final chapter, I address how such an idea applies to the practices of science as a part of that subject matter. Others have written more eloquently than I about the actual teaching of these practices and the scaffolds necessary for ensuring that students, teachers, and teacher educators are able to engage in scientific activity in classrooms.[3] Instead, here I wish to engage with the concerns from thoughtful teachers who remain unconvinced that a different form of teaching is possible, even if it is desirable.

On one side are the school science *realists*, who largely feel that the current model of science teaching in schools—while imperfect—is up to the task of preparing both scientifically literate citizens and future scientists. On the other are the school science *reformers*, who look at the vision of science teaching put forth in documents like the National Research Council's *Framework for K-12 Science Education*, and the Next Generation Science Standards, and see that most science teaching happening today is still quite far from this rich vision of teaching and learning.[4] The reformers, at least in the United States, would claim that science teaching currently does a rather poor job of preparing scientifically literate citizens and future scientists, as evidenced by assessments like NAEP and PISA as well as surveys of public opinion about scientific issues. It is fair to say that both the school science realists and reformers would both welcome a richer vision of science teaching with greater attention to scientific practices. The dilemma of deciding what this looks like in classrooms is rooted in questions concerning the feasibility of change at the scale demanded by the realities of public education.

Before presenting further arguments from each side, I wish to offer a few examples that I have witnessed firsthand that illustrate the current tension between the realist and reformer perspectives of modern science teaching:

- A fourth-grade team in a suburban elementary school ends a unit on electric circuits by having students build "quiz boards" using shoe boxes, metal fasteners, and insulated wire. Students follow step-by-step instructions to build the boxes, along with a component made with a bulb and battery that will light up when students correctly match a question with its answer. The veteran teachers on the team have developed this activity over a decade, and continue to refine it every year.
- In an urban seventh grade physical science classroom, students build rockets powered by Alka-Seltzer tablets in plastic film canisters during a chemical reactions unit. The two teachers in the class have spent an extraordinary

amount of time planning and organizing this activity, which is evident in the engagement of the students in building and designing their rockets. After a single launch of their rockets outside, the students are challenged to change one thing about their design that would make it fly for a longer time. The groups get to work making changes to their rockets—some are changing the fins, amount of water, or placement of the canister—but there is little talk about chemical reactions.

• In a high school environmental science class in a rural community, a teacher sets up a station activity during a unit on soil in which students visit multiple lab tables in order to obtain the information needed to complete a worksheet. It is the day before a long vacation, and the teacher promises a surprise for her students once they have finished the activity. When they are all seated, she brings out a "dirt cake," which is also a model of a soil profile, with a different ingredient for each layer (e.g. the brownie at the bottom represents bedrock, vanilla pudding is the alluvial layer, etc.). After displaying and describing each layer, the teacher instructs the students to complete the problems on the back of the worksheet in groups. When students turn in their work, they receive a piece of the cake.

In sharing these real examples, I want to make clear my respect for these teachers who have applied their creativity and worked very hard to provide their students with rich learning opportunities, sometimes in challenging settings. They also have daily jobs that would sorely vex the patience and skills of a majority of adults. Moreover, it was undeniable that in each classroom the students enjoyed these lessons, were fully engaged in school, and even appeared to learn some science. These were thoughtful teachers trying to do a good job.[5]

My critique is not aimed at the teachers themselves, but at the divergence between the enactment of school science in these classrooms and the practices of real science. What each of these scenes has in common is the veneer of scientific activity—building circuits, modifying the design of rockets, working at lab tables and examining models—yet only the superficial presence of actual scientific practices. To a casual observer passing by the classroom, such activity might look impressive, but to someone seeking evidence of development of students' scientific literacy—namely that students are learning how to think like scientists and engage in a process of knowledge generation—it looks more like playing school.

★★★

The argument from the school science reformer's perspective goes something like this: it is possible and desirable for school science to look a great deal more like real science. Students should investigate authentic questions, use the real tools of scientists, and engage in specific situated practices of knowledge generation as much as possible. Real scientists do not solve problems from textbooks, rather, they access and assemble the information they need to solve a particular problem in a particular context, and students can do the same. Teachers who begin from phenomena, elicit their students' ideas, use those ideas as the basis for instruction, include the collection and analysis of evidence, and afford students the opportunity to craft, present, and defend knowledge claims, will be effective teachers of science.

While it remains important for students to have access to scientific knowledge, the reformers argument continues, it is even more important to put that knowledge to use. Engaging in science practices like developing and revising models, planning and carrying out investigations, developing explanations and arguments from evidence, and engaging in communication about scientific ideas are also quite effective in teaching the science content. Though many of these practices may occur in contemporary science classrooms, they are often deployed in the service of a "right-answer" orientation to teaching science that short-circuits students' opportunities for critical thinking. The school science reformers argue that a more cohesive approach to ensuring that the science practices and subject matter knowledge are learned together will lead to students who are equally well prepared to be either future scientists or scientifically literate non-scientist citizens who will be—in John Dewey's words—able to learn "the ways by which anything is entitled to be called knowledge."[6]

Conversely, the argument from the school realists is as follows: we want real science in our classrooms as much as anyone, but it is more difficult than the reformers suggest. In some sense, this is a problem of scale and resources. Having students engage in science through model-based inquiry, problem-based learning, or even differentiated instruction is very resource-intensive in terms of time, teachers, and materials. While valuable as pedagogical approaches, their use requires a commitment to the work of teaching by the general public that has not been sustained even in the most well-funded schools. There is also a real question about the practicality for a teacher who may see a hundred or more students per day of setting up a classroom in which every student—or even groups of students—are regularly engaged in investigations as either individuals or groups. For better or worse, we have a system of mass education in which teachers are responsible for teaching large groups of students all at the same time. This makes doing real science much more challenging. So do standards and standardized curricula across state, district, and school contexts, that lead to teachers having much less control over what topics are taught and tested.

Further, the school realists argue, the type of teaching in which real science would happen in the classroom requires the presence of a teacher who is practically perfect in every way—like a Mary Poppins version of a science teacher.[7] Such a teacher knows the subject matter well, has an idea of how students learn it, and is a strong enough planner, organizer, and manager to create a successful classroom environment for all students. These teachers do exist, but they are few and far between, and while every teacher may have the capacity to reach this level of expertise, it takes time and effort to do so. In any given population of science teachers, only a small percentage of them are ever going to have the requisite skills necessary to enact this kind of pedagogy in their classrooms, and the best eventually do retire and need to be replaced. Then there is the fact that teaching is simply more difficult in high-need schools for a host of reasons (e.g. no Bunsen burners, school structures that make predicting day-to-day schedules difficult, students with challenging home lives that complicate their school lives, curricula aligned to the majority culture, etc.). A more realistic goal is to teach science practices as they arise naturally in the curriculum, but it is not logistically possible to turn science classrooms into places where students continually engage in scientific practices. Playing school is a necessary compromise in order to teach science—the argument goes—and it works for most.

★★★

While my sympathies lie with the school realists—because teaching is such a difficult job when done well and the reformers' agenda promises to make it even more complex—the evidence suggests that playing school does not in fact work for the vast majority of students. It is a harsh truth for those of us who have spent endless nights crafting lesson plans, grading papers, and laboring over our daily teaching that students are more likely to remember how we made them feel, and less likely to remember the science we thought we taught them.

A former high school science department chair told me the following story in a research interview that illustrates this point. A teacher in his department had run a technologically sophisticated and innovative freshman biology course, and claimed that the students were retaining what they had learned over their subsequent science courses.[8] The chair was somewhat skeptical of these claims, given his own experiences of teaching the same students in later grades. The two colleagues decided to make an experiment out of it, and gathered together a group of 12th graders and gave them the exact test they all had taken and passed with high scores as 9th graders. The results were dismal, and sharing the results with other teachers in the department ultimately led to an overhaul of the school's science curriculum. I wish every school in the country would replicate this experiment, and be equally as wise in not blaming the results on the students.

I wish to echo Dewey here and assert that genuinely teaching students to use the practices of science is an essential component of what it means to educate students in a democracy. Understanding science as a system of human activity implies a degree of control over knowledge construction—not just *what* knowledge, but *whose*—that is necessary in order to make certain that education serves civic ends grounded in principles of democracy and justice.[9]

By ensuring that students understand the basis upon which anything gets to be called knowledge, we build their capacity to begin addressing the major issues of our time—like climate change, nuclear proliferation, global diseases, and the inequitable distribution of resources necessary for human survival—in addition to future problems whose contours we can now scarcely imagine.

I agree with the school science realists that the challenge of truly embedding science practices is much more difficult than the science reformers portray it to be. However, I cast my lot with the school science reformers whose agenda is more consistent with the ambitious, student-centered, and culturally-relevant vision of teaching for which I have advocated throughout this book. In presenting science as a system of human activity, and using its practices as a way to teach the ideas that it has generated, we are providing students with tools to both advance our understanding of the natural and human-made world, as well as the opportunity to put that knowledge to work in efforts to craft a more just society.

Notes

1 An outstanding example of this phenomenon is evident in the ethnographic study of a high school biology class by Reba Page (1999), in which she writes, "I was struck by this broad pattern across the nine classes in which I observed, where teachers and students seemed to be holding science at bay rather than engaging in the construction of scholastic and social relationships centered around subject matter," (p. 559).
2 I have intentionally avoided terms like pedagogical content knowledge (Shulman, 1987), and didactic transposition (Bosch & Gascón, 2006) because frankly—even as labels—they come laden with a great deal of theoretical baggage that only obscures my argument. I use the term "access" here in the spirit of John Goodlad and his vision outlined in the Agenda for Education in a Democracy project (Goodlad et al., 2004), in which one of the four core principles for education is "access to knowledge."
3 Mark Windschitl, Jessica Thompson, and other science educators working from the University of Washington-Seattle have collectively produced an impressive body of work on this topic. See for example: Stroupe & Gotwals, 2017; Thompson, Hagenah, Lohwasser, & Laxton, 2015; Windschitl & Calabrese Barton, 2016; Windschitl et al., 2008; Windschitl, Thompson, & Braaten, 2009; Windschitl, Thompson, Braaten, & Stroupe, 2012; Windschitl & Thompson, 2013.
4 Achieve Inc., 2013; National Research Council, 2012.
5 These are definitely not classrooms where Haberman's (1991) notorious "pedagogy of poverty" is happening.
6 See Rudolph (2014) for a thoughtful discussion of Dewey's continued relevance for science teachers in an analysis of his century old address to the annual meeting of the American Association for the Advancement of Science (Dewey, 1910)
7 Mary Poppins is a fictional white British nanny created by author P. L. Travers in the 1930s and later popularized in the Walt Disney film of the same name. She is described as "practically perfect in every way." This description is relative however, because early editions of the books required substantial revision over time when racist depictions of characters within them did not age well. Therefore, while a critical theorist might pose the question, "practically perfect for who?", from the perspective of reformed science teaching we can invoke Mary Poppins as a reasonable (but imperfect) first approximation model of a practically perfect teacher.

8 The story of the subsequent development and implementation of the truly innovative and teacher-authored introductory high school science curriculum that followed these events is recounted as a case study in Larkin, Seyforth, and Lasky (2009).

9 An excellent example of this idea in practice can be found in the study by Miller and Roehrig (2018), which describes a school's project to repurpose a historically common indigenous game of "snow snakes" to teach engineering principles. This effort appealed to the aspirations for more culture–school connections within the Ojibwe community where the school was located.

AFTERWORD

Good Reasons for Becoming a Science Teacher

I remember very clearly the early-morning commercials for the U.S. Peace Corps that I saw as a kid in the 1970s that ended with the tagline, "the toughest job you'll ever love." These ads, along with the Army slogan "Be all that you can be," (which I also saw on television around that time) planted the idea of doing something with my life that was both personally rewarding and larger than myself. In the 1990s, I actually did become a Peace Corps volunteer, and left New Jersey to teach science and mathematics in secondary schools in Kenya and Papua New Guinea. The ad was right; it was tough, and I loved it.

I think about those Peace Corps commercials quite a bit now in my work as a professor in preparing teachers for middle and high school science classrooms. Many of my students have the same sense of aspiration and purpose evoked in those Peace Corps ads, but their total impact on our society is tempered by the harsh reality that there are simply not enough new science teachers to meet the demand. On those days when our admissions numbers are looking low and science teacher scholarships go unclaimed yet again for lack of applicants, I wish that there were more spirited public messages about the significance of becoming a science teacher. Here is my attempt to make one.

People love science for many reasons, but for far too long school science has served as a way to sort and exclude, as if only certain people could benefit from what science has to offer. Recent reforms in science education—embodied in the Next Generation Science Standards—are genuinely exciting for people like me who see science as a way to understand the world. Often, school science is portrayed and experienced as the controlled delivery of facts, but this new vision puts real world phenomena, scientific practices and students' thinking at the core of learning scientific concepts.

It seems certain that people who become science teachers over the next decade will approach teaching science in very different ways from how they learned it themselves as students in school. For people whose own school science experiences left them discouraged, even as they maintained a love for science itself, becoming a science teacher provides the opportunity to make science more accessible and meaningful for a whole new generation of students.

What makes a good teacher different from any other educated adult? Of course, they know their content, but good teachers also anticipate the different paths that students will take to learn a particular concept. Good teachers study their students to better understand how their lives influence their learning. Good teachers know that they are autonomous professionals who draw upon the wisdom of practice, research, and their colleagues and are capable of making thousands of decisions each day to meet the learning needs of their students. Good teachers regularly wrestle with the meaning of public education in a democracy. They know when to press both their students and administrators on issues of fairness and equity, and they understand that democracy requires deliberation and negotiation, and also sometimes being that lone voice of dissent to raise important but uncomfortable issues to those in power. Good teachers walk their talk because their students expect no less.

Many science-minded individuals who have let their interests and talents take them in other directions for a first career often find the second career of teaching immensely satisfying, even when it is difficult. Challenges to being a good science teacher can come from many directions: the bureaucracy of schools, the needs of students and parents, and the complexity of the subject matter itself. The small daily victories of making genuine connections with students as people, kindling their interest in the world around them and fostering lasting scientific understandings more than compensate for the effort.

Now more than ever, the impact of science teaching will be felt long into the future because good science teachers make it possible for others to engage productively in the affairs of science, even if students do not all become scientists themselves. Those who choose to become science teachers will be able to equip students to fight the effects of climate change, reverse centuries of environmental degradation, and redesign the way we use energy on our planet. Our students will use what they learn in our science classes to find better ways to keep people healthy, improve our quality of life, and create a more just society. And, even if we do not end up traveling to the moon or Mars ourselves, it is possible that our students will.

The choice to teach science is also a step toward becoming a part of something larger than just a single person. The work of science teaching has both tangible and immeasurable rewards, simple pleasures, and a type of personal fulfilment simply not found elsewhere. My humble request is that more people consider the possibility of science teaching as a career and think about the impact that they could make—in schools, in our world and on each other—by deciding to become a science teacher.

REFERENCES

Abell, S. K. (2007). Research on Science Teacher Knowledge. In S. K. Abell & N. G. Lederman (Eds.), *Handbook of Research on Science Education* (pp. 1105–1150). Mahwah, N.J.: Lawrence Erlbaum Associates.

Achieve Inc. (2013). *Next Generation Science Standards: For States, By States*. Washington, DC: National Academies Press.

Alvarez, L. W., Alvarez, W., Asaro, F., & Michel, H. V. (1980). Extraterrestrial Cause for the Cretaceous-Tertiary Extinction. *Science, 208*(4448), 1095–1108.

American Chemical Society. (2012). *Chemistry in the Community: Chemcom* (6th ed.). New York, NY: W.H. Freeman and Co./BFW.

Bang, M., Warren, B., Rosebery, A. S., & Medin, D. (2013). Desettling Expectations in Science Education. *Human Development*, 55(5–6), 302–318. doi:10.1159/000345322

Banks, J. A. (1995). Multicultural Education: Historical Development, Dimensions, and Practice. In J. A. Banks & C. A. M. Banks (Eds.), *Handbook of Research on Multicultural Education* (pp. 3–24). New York, NY: Macmillan.

Bosch, M., & Gascón, J. (2006). Twenty-five Years of the Didactic Transposition. *ICMI Bulletin*, 58, 51–65.

Branch, G., & Mead, L. S. (2008). "Theory" in Theory and Practice. *Evolution: Education and Outreach*, 1(3), 287–289.

Bransford, J. D., Brown, A. L., & Cocking, R. R. (Eds.). (1999). *How People Learn: Brain, Mind, Experience, and School*. Washington, DC: National Academy Press.

Britzman, D. P. (2003). *Practice Makes Practice: A Critical Study of Learning to Teach* (Rev. ed.). Albany, NY: State University of New York Press.

Brown, B. A. (2006). "It Isn't No Slang that can be Said about This Stuff": Language, Identity, and Appropriating Science Discourse. *Journal of Research in Science Teaching*, 43(1), 96–126. doi:10.1002/tea.20096

Brown, B. A., & Spang, E. (2008). Double Talk: Synthesizing Everyday and Science Language in the Classroom. *Science Education*, 92(4), 708–732.

Brown, J. S., Collins, A., & Duguid, P. (1989). Situated Cognition and the Culture of Learning. *Educational Researcher*, 18(1), 32–42.

Bybee, R. W. (1987). Science Education and the Science-Technology-Society (S-T-S) Theme. *Science Education*, 71(5), 667–683.

Calabrese Barton, A. (2003). *Teaching Science for Social Justice*. New York, NY: Teachers College Press.

Chambers, D. W. (1983). Stereotypic Images of the Scientist: The Draw-A-Scientist Test. *Science Education*, 67(2), 255–265. doi:10.1002/sce.3730670213

Collins, H. M., & Pinch, T. J. (1998). *The Golem: What You Should Know About Science* (2nd ed.). New York, NY: Cambridge University Press.

Conant, J. B. (1951). *Science and Common Sense*. New Haven, CT: Yale University Press.

Cuban, L. (1989). The 'At-risk' Label and the Problem of Urban School Reform. *Phi Delta Kappan*, 70(10), 780–801.

Cuban, L. (2013). *Inside the Black Box of Classroom Practice: Change Without Reform in American Education*. Cambridge, MA: Harvard Education Publishing Group.

Danielson, C. (2007). *Enhancing Professional Practice: A Framework for Teaching* (2nd ed.). Alexandria, V.A..: Association for Supervision and Curriculum Development.

Delisle, J. (2015). Differentiation Doesn't Work. *Education Week*, 34(15), 28, 36.

Dewey, J. (1910). Science as Subject-Matter and as Method. *Science*, 31(787), 121–127.

Dimick, A. S. (2012). Student Empowerment in an Environmental Science Classroom: Toward a Framework for Social Justice Science Education. *Science Education*, 96(6), 990–1012. doi:10.1002/sce.21035

Du Bois, W. E. B. (1903/1993). *The Souls of Black Folk*. New York, NY: Knopf.

Duschl, R. A., & Grandy, R. E. (2008). Reconsidering the Character and Role of Inquiry in School Science: Framing the Debates. In R. A. Duschl & R. E. Grandy (Eds.), *Teaching scientific inquiry* (pp. 1–37). Rotterdam, The Netherlands: Sense Publishers.

Dweck, C. S. (2006). *Mindset: The New Psychology of Success* (1st ed.). New York, NY: Random House.

Eschtruth, A. K., Evans, R. A., & Battles, J. J. (2013). Patterns and Predictors of Survival in Tsuga Canadensis Populations Infested by the Exotic Pest Adelges Tsugae: 20 Years of Monitoring. *Forest Ecology and Management*, 305, 195–203. doi:10.1016/j.foreco.2013.05.047

Faber, A., & Mazlish, E. (2008). *How to Talk so Kids can Learn*. New York: Simon and Schuster.

Faraday, M. (1938). The Chemical History of a Candle. *Harvard classics*. (Vol. 30, pp. 86–172). New York, NY: P. F. Collier.

Fenstermacher, G. D., & Richardson, V. (2005). On Making Determinations of Quality in Teaching. *Teachers College Record*, 107(1), 186–213.

Freire, P. (1970). *Pedagogy of the Oppressed*. New York, NY: Herder and Herder.

Freire, P. (1985). *The Politics of Education: Culture, Power, and Liberation*. South Hadley, Mass.: Bergin & Garvey.

Fricker, M. (2007). *Epistemic Injustice: Power and the Ethics Of Knowing*. Oxford; New York, NY: Oxford University Press.

Gardner, H. (1999). *Intelligence Reframed: Multiple Intelligences for the 21st Century*. New York, NY: Basic Books.

Gee, J. P. (2003). *What Video Games Have to Teach us about Learning and Literacy* (1st ed.). New York, NY: Palgrave/Macmillan.

Gerta, K., Paula, M., Jahnavi, P., et al. (2018). Environmental Changes During the Cretaceous-Paleogene Mass Extinction and Paleocene-Eocene Thermal Maximum: Implications for the Anthropocene. *Gondwana Research*, 56: 69–89.

Gieryn, T. F. (1999). *Cultural Boundaries of Science: Credibility on the Line*. Chicago, IL: University of Chicago Press.

González, N., Moll, L. C., & Amanti, C. (2005). *Funds of Knowledge: Theorizing Practices in Households, Communities, and Classrooms*. Mahwah, NJ: L. Erlbaum Associates.

Goodlad, J. I., Mantle-Bromley, C., & Goodlad, S. J. (2004). *Education for Everyone: Agenda for Education in a Democracy*. Indianapolis, IN: Jossey-Bass.

Grant, C. A., & Sleeter, C. E. (1985). The Literature on Multicultural Education: Review and Analysis. *Educational Review*, 37(2), 97–118.

Haber-Schaim, U., Cutting, R., Kirksey, H. G., & Pratt, H. (1999). *Introductory Physical Science*. Lakewood, CO: Science Curriculum, Incorporated.

Haberman, M. (1991). The Pedagogy of Poverty Versus Good Teaching. *Phi Delta Kappan*, 73(4), 290–294.

Haberman, M., Gillette, M., & Hill, D. A. (2018). *Star Teachers of Children in Poverty* (2nd ed.). New York, NY: Routledge.

Hammerness, K., Darling-Hammond, L., Bransford, J., et al. (2005). How Teachers Learn and Develop. In L. Darling-Hammond & J. Bransford (Eds.), *Preparing Teachers for a Changing World: What Teachers Should Learn and be Able to Do* (1st ed., pp. 358–389). San Francisco, CA: Jossey-Bass.

Haraway, D. J. (1989). *Primate Visions: Gender, Race, and Nature in the World of Modern Science*. New York, NY: Routledge.

Harvard-Smithsonian Center for Astrophysics, & Annenberg/CPB Project. (2000). Learning To Share Perspectives. Looking at Learning … again. Part 2 [videorecording]. Cambridge, Mass: Smithsonian Astrophysical Observatory, Harvard-Smithsonian Center for Astrophysics.

Hattie, J. (2009). *Visible Learning: A Synthesis of over 800 Meta-Analyses Relating to Achievement*. London; New York, NY: Routledge.

Hewson, P. W., Beeth, M. E., & Thorley, N. R. (1998). Teaching For Conceptual Change. In B. J. Fraser & K. G. Tobin (Eds.), *International Handbook Of Science Education* (pp. 199–218). Dordrecht, The Netherlands: Kluwer Academic Publishers.

Hofstadter, D. R., & Sander, E. (2013). *Surfaces and Essences: Analogy as the Fuel and Fire of Thinking*. New York, NY: Basic Books.

Howard, G. R. (2006). *We Can't Teach What We Don't Know: White Teachers, Multiracial Schools* (2nd ed.). New York, NY: Teachers College Press.

Hudicourt-Barnes, J. (2003). The Use Of Argumentation in Haitian Creole Science Classrooms. *Harvard Educational Review*, 73(1), 73–93.

Kahneman, D. (2011). *Thinking, Fast and Slow* (1st ed.). New York, NY: Farrar, Straus and Giroux.

Kennedy, M. M. (2010). Attribution Error and the Quest for Teacher Quality. *Educational Researcher*, 39(8), 591–598. doi:10.3102/0013189X10390804

Kuhn, T. S. (1970). *The Structure of Scientific Revolutions* (2nd, enl. ed.). Chicago, IL: University of Chicago Press.

Ladson-Billings, G. (1994). *The Dreamkeepers: Successful Teachers of African American Children* (1st ed.). San Francisco: Jossey-Bass Publishers.

Ladson-Billings, G. (1995). Towards a Theory of Culturally Relevant Pedagogy. *American Educational Research Journal*, 32(3), 465–491.

Ladson-Billings, G. (2000). Racialized Discourses and Ethnic Epistemologies. In N. Denzin & Y. Lincoln (Eds.), *Handbook of Qualitative Research* (Second edition ed.). Thousand Oaks, CA: Sage.

Ladson-Billings, G. (2006). "Yes, But How Do We Do It?": Practicing Culturally Relevant Pedagogy. In J. Landsman & C. W. Lewis (Eds.), *White Teachers, Diverse Classrooms: A Guide to Building Inclusive Schools, Promoting High Expectations, and Eliminating Racism* (1st ed., pp. 29–42). Sterling, VA: Stylus Pub.

Ladson-Billings, G. (2014). Culturally Relevant Pedagogy 2.0: A.K.A. The Remix. *Harvard Educational Review*, 84(1), 74–84.

Larkin, D. B. (2010). *Learning the Pedagogical Implications of Student Diversity: The Lived Experiences of Preservice Teachers Learning to Teach Secondary Science in Diverse Classrooms.* Unpublished doctoral dissertation, University of Wisconsin-Madison, Madison, Wisconsin.

Larkin, D. B. (2012). Misconceptions About "Misconceptions": Preservice Secondary Science Teachers' Views on the Value and Role of Student Ideas. *Science Education*, 96(5), 927–959. doi:10.1002/sce.21022.

Larkin, D. B. (2013). *Deep knowledge: Learning to teach science for understanding and equity.* New York, NY: Teachers College Press.

Larkin, D. B., Seyforth, S. C., & Lasky, H. J. (2009). Implementing and sustaining science curriculum reform: A study of leadership practices among teachers within a high school science department. *Journal of Research in Science Teaching*, 4(7), 813–835. doi:10.1002/tea.20291.

Latour, B., & Woolgar, S. (1979). *Laboratory Life: The Social Construction of Scientific Facts.* Beverly Hills: Sage Publications.

Lee, B. (1971). Liberate Yourself from Classical Karate. Black Belt, 9(9), 24–27.

Lewis, J., & D'Orso, M. (1999). *Walking With the Wind: A Memoir of the Movement* (1st Harvest ed.). San Diego: Harcourt Brace.

Louv, R. (2005). *Last Child in the Woods: Saving Our Children from Nature-Deficit Disorder* (1st ed.). Chapel Hill, NC: Algonquin Books of Chapel Hill.

Maimon, G. (1999). Little Pigs and Big Ideas: Blowing Down The 'At-Risk' Straw House. *International Journal of Leadership in Education*, 2(3), 191–205.

Martin, J. L., & Beese, J. A. (2017). Talking Back at School: Using the Literacy Classroom as a Site for Resistance to the School-to-prison Pipeline and Recognition of Students Labeled "At-Risk". *Urban Education*, 52(10), 1204–1232. doi:10.1177/0042085915602541.

McKie, R. (2010, 3 April). Henrietta Lacks's Cells Were Priceless, But Her Family Can't Afford a Hospital, *The Observer*. Retrieved from https://www.theguardian.com/world/2010/apr/04/henrietta-lacks-cancer-cells.

Meier, D. (1995). How Our Schools Could Be. *Phi Delta Kappan*, 76(5), 369–373.

Merritt, J., Mi Yeon, L., Rillero, P., & Kinach, B. M. (2017). Problem-Based Learning in K-8 Mathematics and Science Education: A Literature Review. *Interdisciplinary Journal of Problem-based Learning*, 11(2), 1–12. doi:10.7771/1541–5015.1674

MET project. (2012). *Gathering Feedback for Teaching: Combining High-Quality Observations with Student Surveys and Achievement Gains.* The Bill and Melinda Gates Foundation. Retrieved January 31, 2012 from http://www.gatesfoundation.org

Mettler, K. (2016, 23 Jun). "Good Trouble": How John Lewis Fuses New and Old Tactics to Teach about Civil Disobedience, *The Washington Post*. Retrieved from https://www.washingtonpost.com/news/morning-mix/wp/2016/06/23/good-trouble-how-john-lewis-fuses-new-and-old-tactics-to-teach-about-civil-disobedience

Meyer, A., Rose, D. H., & Gordon, D. (2016). *Universal Design for Learning: Theory and Practice*. Wakefield, MA: CAST Professional Publishing.

Miller, B. G., & Roehrig, G. (2018). Indigenous Cultural Contexts for Stem Experiences: Snow Snakes' Impact on Students and the Community. *Cultural Studies of Science Education*, 13(1), 31–58. doi:10.1007/s11422–11016–9738–9734.

Miller, D. I., Nolla, K. M., Eagly, A. H., & Uttal, D. H. (2018). The Development of Children's Gender-Science Stereotypes: A Meta-Analysis of 5 Decades Of U.S. Draw-A-Scientist Studies. *Child Development*, 89(6), 1943–1955. doi:10.1111/cdev.13039.

Miller, E., Manz, E., Russ, R., Stroupe, D., & Berland, L. (2018). Addressing the Epistemic Elephant in the Room: Epistemic Agency and the Next Generation Science Standards. *Journal of Research in Science Teaching*, 55(7), 1053–1075. doi:10.1002/tea.21459.

Morales-Doyle, D. (2017). Justice-Centered Science Pedagogy: A Catalyst for Academic Achievement and Social Transformation. *Science Education*, 101(6), 1034–1060. doi:10.1002/sce.21305.

Morris, E. (2018). *The Ashtray (Or the Man Who Denied Reality)*. Chicago, IL; London: The University of Chicago Press.

National Board of Professional Teaching Standards. (2016). *What Teachers Should Know and Be Able to Do*. Arlington, VA: National Board of Professional Teaching Standards. Retrieved from http://accomplishedteacher.org/wp-content/uploads/2016/12/NBPTS-What-Teachers-Should-Know-and-Be-Able-to-Do-.pdf

National Research Council. (2002). *Minority Students in Special and Gifted Education*. Washington, DC: National Academies Press.

National Research Council. (2006). *America's Lab Report: Investigations in High School science*. Washington, DC:National Academies Press.

National Research Council. (2007). Taking Science to School: Learning and Teaching Science in Grades K-8. In R. A. Duschl, H. A. Schweingruber, A. W. Shouse & Committee on Science. *Learning Kindergarten Through Eighth Grade*. (Eds.). Washington, DC: National Academies Press. Retrieved from http://books.nap.edu/openbook.php?isbn=0309102057

National Research Council. (2012). *A Framework for K-12 Science Education: Practices, Crosscutting Concepts, and Core Ideas*. Washington, DC: The National Academies Press.

O'Neil, C. (2016). *Weapons of Math Destruction: How Big Data Increases Inequality and Threatens Democracy*. New York, NY: Crown.

Oakes, J. (2005). *Keeping Track: How Schools Structure Inequality* (2nd ed.). New Haven, CT: Yale University Press.

Page, R. N. (1999). The Uncertain Value of School Knowledge: Biology at Westridge High. *Teachers College Record*, 100(3), 554–601.

Pajares, M. F. (1992). Teachers' Beliefs and Educational Research: Cleaning Up a Messy Construct. *Review of Educational Research*, 62(3), 307–332.

Pease, M. A., & Kuhn, D. (2011). Experimental Analysis of the Effective Components of Problem-Based Learning. *Science Education*, 95(1), 57–86. doi:10.1002/sce.20412.

Perkins, D. (1998). What Is Understanding? In M. S. Wiske (Ed.), *Teaching for Understanding: Linking Research with Practice* (1st ed.). San Francisco: Jossey-Bass Publishers.

Plato, Tredennick, H., & Tarrant, H. (1993). *The Last Days of Socrates*. London, England; New York, NY: Penguin Books.

Popkewitz, T. S. (1987). *The Formation of School Subjects: The Struggle for Creating An American Institution*. New York, NY: Falmer Press.

Posner, G. J., Strike, K. A., Hewson, P. W., & Gertzog, W. A. (1982). Accommodation of a Scientific Conception: Toward a Theory of Conceptual Change. *Science Education*, 66 (2), 211–227.

Rees, P. (Writer). (17 Oct 2003). Penny drop [Television series episode]. In Beyond Entertainment (Producer), Mythbusters. Silver Spring, MD: Discovery Channel.

Rudolph, J. L. (2002). *Scientists in the Classroom: The Cold War Reconstruction of American Science Education* (1st ed.). New York, NY: Palgrave Macmillan.

Rudolph, J. L. (2014). Dewey's "Science as Method" A Century Later: Reviving Science Education For Civic Ends. *American Educational Research Journal*, 51(6), 1056–1083. doi:10.3102/0002831214554277.

Sadler, P. M., Sonnert, G., Coyle, H. P., Cook-Smith, N., & Miller, J. L. (2013). The Influence of Teachers' Knowledge on Student Learning in Middle School Physical Science Classrooms. *American Educational Research Journal*, 50(5), 1020–1049.

Sadler, T. D., & Zeidler, D. L. (2004). The Morality of Socioscientific Issues: Construal and Resolution of Genetic Engineering Dilemmas. *Science Education*, 88(1), 4–27.

Scerri, E. R. (2013). *A Tale of Seven Elements.* New York, NY: Oxford University Press.

Shulman, L. S. (1987). Knowledge and Teaching: Foundations of the New Reform. *Harvard Educational Review*, 57(1), 1–22.

Sizer, T. R. (1984). *Horace's Compromise: The Dilemma of the American High School: The First Report From a Study Of High Schools, Co-Sponsored by the National Association of Secondary School Principals and the Commission on Educational Issues of the National Association of Independent Schools.* Boston: Houghton Mifflin.

Sizer, T. R. (1992). *Horace's School: Redesigning the American High School.* Boston: Houghton Mifflin Co.

Skloot, R. (2010). *The Immortal Life of Henrietta Lacks.* New York, NY: Crown Publishers.

Sleeter, C. E. (1993). How White Teachers Construct Race. In C. McCarthy & W. Crichlow (Eds.), *Race, Identity and Representation in Education* (pp. 157–171). New York, NY: Routledge.

Sleeter, C. E. (1994). White Racism. *Multicultural Education*, 1(4), 5.

Sleeter, C. E. (2001a). Epistemological Diversity in Research on Preservice Teacher Preparation for Historically Underserved Children. *Review of Research in Education*, 25, 209–250.

Sleeter, C. E. (2001b). Preparing Teachers for Culturally Diverse Schools: Research and The Overwhelming Presence of Whiteness. *Journal of Teacher Education*, 52(2), 94–106.

Sleeter, C. E. (2015). *White Bread: Weaving Cultural Past into the Present.* Rotterdam: SensePublishers.

Smilie. (2008). *Crazy Asian War.* Philadelphia, PA: Xlibris.

Smith, J. P., diSessa, A. A., & Roschelle, J. (1993). Misconceptions Reconceived: A Constructivist Analysis of Knowledge in Transition. *The Journal of the Learning Sciences*, 3(2), pp. 115–163

Snively, G., & Corsiglia, J. (2001). Discovering Indigenous Science: Implications for Science Education. *Science Education*, 85, 6–34.

Sparks, S. (2015). Differentiated Instruction: A Primer. *Education Week*, 34(20).

Speed, S. A., Bradley, E., & Garland, K. V. (2015). Teaching Adult Learner Characteristics and Facilitation Strategies Through Simulation-Based Practice. *Journal of Educational Technology Systems*, 44(2), 203.

Spencer, M. B. (2008). Lessons Learned and Opportunities Ignored Since Brown V. Board Of Education: Youth Development and the Myth Of A Color-Blind Society. *Educational Researcher*, 37(5), 253–266. doi:10.3102/0013189x08322767

Steele, C. (2010). *Whistling Vivaldi: And Other Clues to how Stereotypes Affect Us* (1st ed.). New York, NY: W.W. Norton & Company.

Strike, K. A., & Posner, G. J. (1992). A Revisionist Theory of Conceptual Change. In R. A. Duschl & R. J. Hamilton (Eds.), *Philosophy of Science, Cognitive Psychology, And Educational Theory and Practice.* Albany: State University of New York Press.

Stroupe, D., & Gotwals, A. W. (2017). "It's 1000 Degrees in Here When I Teach": Providing Preservice Teachers with an Extended Opportunity to Approximate Ambitious Instruction. *Journal of Teacher Education*, 69(3), 294–306. doi:0022487117709742.

Thompson, J., Hagenah, S., Lohwasser, K., & Laxton, K. (2015). Problems Without Ceilings. *Journal of Teacher Education*, 66(4), 363–381. doi:10.1177/0022487115592462.

Tomlinson, C. A. (1999). *The Differentiated Classroom: Responding to the Needs of all Learners.* Alexandria, VA: Association for Supervision and Curriculum Development.

Tomlinson, C. A., & McTighe, J. (2006). *Integrating Differentiated Instruction & Understanding by Design: Connecting Content and Kids.* Alexandria, VA: Association for Supervision and Curriculum Development.

Upadhyay, B. (2009). Teaching Science for Empowerment in an Urban Classroom: A Case Study of a Hmong Teacher. *Equity & Excellence in Education*, 42(2), 217–232. doi:10.1080/10665680902779366.

Villegas, A. M., & Davis, D. (2008). Preparing Teachers of Color to Confront Racial/Ethnic Disparities on Educational Outcomes. In M. Cochran-Smith, S. Feiman-Nemser, D. J. McIntyre & Association of Teacher Educators. (Eds.), *Handbook of Research on Teacher Education: Enduring Questions in Changing Contexts* (3rd ed., pp. 583–605). New York, NY: Routledge; Co-published by the Association of Teacher Educators.

Villegas, A. M., & Lucas, T. (2002). Preparing Culturally Responsive Teachers: Rethinking the Curriculum. *Journal of Teacher Education*, 53(1), 20–32.

Wachter-Boettcher, S. (2017). *Technically Wrong: Sexist Apps, Biased Algorithms, and Other Threats of Toxic Tech* (First edition. ed.). New York, NY: W. W. Norton & Company.

Warren, B., Ballenger, C., Ogonowski, M., Rosebery, A. S., & Hudicourt-Barnes, J. (2001). Rethinking Diversity in Learning Science: The Logic of Everyday Sense-Making. *Journal of Research in Science Teaching*, 38(5), 529–552.

Wiggins, G. P., & McTighe, J. (1998). *Understanding by Design.* Alexandria, VA: Association for Supervision and Curriculum Development.

Willingham, D. T., Hughes, E. M., & Dobolyi, D. G. (2015). The Scientific Status of Learning Styles Theories. *Teaching of Psychology*, 42(3), 266–271.

Windschitl, M. (2003). Inquiry Projects in Science Teacher Education: What Can Investigative Experiences Reveal about Teacher Thinking and Eventual Classroom Practice? *Science Education*, 87(1), 112.

Windschitl, M. (2004). Folk Theories of "Inquiry:" How Preservice Teachers Reproduce the Discourse and Practices of an Atheoretical Scientific Method. *Journal of Research in Science Teaching*, 41(5), 481–512.

Windschitl, M., & Calabrese Barton, A. (2016). Rigor and Equity by Design: Seeking A Core of Practices for the Science Education Community. In D. H. Gitomer & C. A. Bell (Eds.), *Aera Handbook of Research on Teaching* (5th ed., pp. 1099–1158). Washington, DC: American Educational Research Association.

Windschitl, M., Thompson, J., & Braaten, M. (2008). Beyond the Scientific Method: Model-Based Inquiry as Aa New Paradigm of Preference for School Science Investigations. *Science Education*, 92(5), 941–967.

Windschitl, M., Thompson, J., & Braaten, M. (2009). *Fostering Ambitious Pedagogy in Novice Teachers: The New Role of Tool-Supported Analyses of Student Work.*, Paper presented at the Annual meeting of the National Association for Research in Science Teaching. Garden Grove, CA.

Windschitl, M., Thompson, J., Braaten, M., & Stroupe, D. (2012). Proposing a Core Set of Instructional Practices and Tools for Teachers of Science. *Science Education*, 96(5), 878–903. doi:10.1002/sce.21027.

Windschitl, M., & Thompson, J. J. (2013). The Modeling Toolkit. *Science Teacher*, 80(6), 63–69.

Windschitl, M., Thompson, J. J., & Braaten, M. L. (2018). *Ambitious Science Teaching.* Cambridge, MA: Harvard Educational Press.

Wormeli, R. (2018). *Fair Isn't Always Equal: Assessing & Grading in the Differentiated Classroom.* Portsmouth, NH: Stenhouse Publishers.

Yager, R. E. (1993). Science-technology-Society as Reform. *School Science and Mathematics*, 93(3), 145–151. doi:10.1111/j.1949–8594.1993.tb12213.

Zeichner, K., & Conklin, H. (2005). Teacher Education Programs. In AERA Panel on Research and Teacher Education, M. Cochran-Smith & K. Zeichner (Eds.), *Studying Teacher Education: The Report of the Aera Panel on Research and Teacher Education* (pp. 645–736). Mahwah, N.J.: Published for the American Educational Research Association by Lawrence Erlbaum Associates.

Zeichner, K., & Gore, J. (1990). Teacher Socialization. In W. R. Houston (Ed.), *Handbook of Research on Teacher Education* (pp. 329–348). New York, NY: Macmillan.

Zeidler, D. L., Sadler, T. D., Simmons, M. L., & Howes, E. V. (2005). Beyond Sts: A Research-Based Framework for Socioscientific Issues Education. *Science Education*, 89(3), 357–377. doi:10.1002/sce.20048.

Zhai, L. (2019). Illuminating the Enactment of High-Leverage Teaching Practices in an Exemplary World Language Teaching Video Library. *American Educational Research Journal*,. doi:10.3102/0002831218824289.

INDEX

Note: page references with 'n' indicates chapter notes.

Faber, A. 59n6
fairness 13
Faraday, Michael 79
Fenstermacher, G. D. 103n3
field trips 64–67, 66–67nn5–11;
  environmental education through 71–73
fraud, feeling like a 105–7, 110, 111
Freire, Paolo 39n8, 70, 75n5
fundamental attribution error 84
Funds of Knowledge project 76n9

Gardner, Howard 74
Gee, J. P. 111n4
Gieryn, T. F. 53n2
goggles 55–59, 59nn2–7
Goodlad, John 118n2
good teachers 3, 121
good trouble 3, 5n3, 9
Grandy, R. E. 48n11
grouping students 100–101
growth *see* professional growth
guest speakers 61–64, 66n1–4

H., Mr. 97
Haberman, M. 118n5
Haber-Schaim, Uri 47n6
Haraway, D. J. 53n2
HeLa cells 35–39

individualized educational plans (IEPs) 98,
  99; assessments 101, 104n8; *see also*
  differentiated instruction
inference 80, 81
interpretation 80–86

judgement 80–86
justice 13
justice-centered approach (teaching science
  for social justice) 37

knowledge: access to 1, 3, 18, 41–42, 65,
  98, 99, 118n2; construction 108,
  117–18; critical approaches to
  52–53, 53n2
Kopp, Kevin 71
Kuhn, T. S. 14n2, 53n2

lab reports 45
labs 40–48, 47–48nn8–12, 47n6, 47nn2–3;
  safety 55–60, 59nn2–7; *see also*
  classrooms
Ladson-Billings, Gloria 10, 12,
  14, 14n1

languages 12–13; English learners 40, 76n9,
  94, 98, 99
Latour, B. 53n2
learning plans, students' own 102
learning styles 15n8
lectures 92, 95n9
Lenz's Law 19, 20n7
lesson planning 92–93
Lewis, John 3, 5n2
lists of things to learn 108–9, 111n7
Louv, Richard 69, 70, 74, 75, 75n2

Mazlish, E. 59n6
McTighe, Jay 38n3
Meier, Deborah 38n3
mentoring new science teachers 88–95,
  95nn1–2, 96n8–9; suggestions (1–10)
  90–95
Merritt, J. 39n6
Middlecamp, Cathy 39n10
Miller, B. G. 119n9
misconceptions, students' 21–23, 23n1
model-based inquiry 10, 14n2, 40–48,
  48n11, 50, 53n3, 116; revising simple
  models 50–53, 53nn2–4; use of
  simulations 49–52
Morris, E. 14n2
MOSART project report 20n2

National Academy of Science 42
National Board of Professional Teaching
  Standards 103n1
National Research Council, *Framework for
  K-12 Science Education* 114
naturalist intelligence 73–76
nature deficit disorders 68–76, 75nn1–8,
  76n9; community resources for 71–73;
  diagnosing 69–70; environmental
  education for 70–71; naturalist
  intelligence, cultivating 73–76
Next Generation Science Standards
  (NGSS) 3, 5n2, 47n1, 114, 120
Nisga'a people 59n8
novice teachers *see* pre-service teachers

observations 79–87, 86n1–7, 87n8,
  87n10–15; as term 80–82

Page, Reba 118n1
perfection 110–11, 116–17, 118n7
performance-oriented teaching
  94–95, 95n8
Perkins, D. 111n3

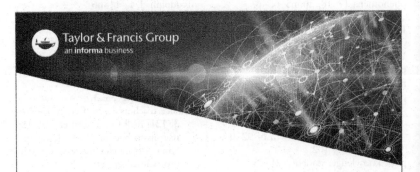